How to Teach Academic Vocabulary

By Dr. Sharon Faber

Incentive Publications, Inc.
Nashville, Tennessee

Illustrations by Kathleen Bullock
Cover by Robert Voigts
Edited by Jill Norris and Marjorie Frank
Copyedited by Cary Grayson

ISBN 978-0-86530-249-5

1   2   3   4   5   6   7   8   9   10   13   12   11   10

Printed by Sheridan Books, Inc., Chelsea, Michigan • June 2010
www.incentivepublications.com

Contents

Chapter 1
The Research on Vocabulary

Chapter 2
What Is Academic Vocabulary?

Chapter 3
A Nifty Fifty—Vocabulary Strategies, Activities, and Games

Chapter 4
Teaching the Strategies, Activities, and Games

How to Teach Academic Vocabulary So Kids Will Remember

> "*The aim [of education] must be the training of independently acting and thinking individuals who, however, see in the service to the community their highest life achievement.*"
>
> – *Albert Einstein*

There are a few things that I've learned about education and educators over the years, and I want to share some of them with you before I give you any ideas on teaching vocabulary. Understanding my philosophy of life and education will provide you with the prior knowledge you need to understand my thinking. So, here's what I think:

- Anyone who has been an educator for ten years or more realizes that education is cyclical. What goes around generally comes back around (but often with a new name which districts then use as new initiatives).

- Teaching at any level is always a work in progress, and teachers should remember that learning to teach is a gradual process. The concerns and problems we face as teachers change as we gain more experience in the classroom.

- During the beginning years as classroom teachers, our attention tends to be focused on survival. How to maintain discipline, motivate students, evaluate student work, and deal with parents are universal concerns as we begin our teaching careers.

- As we gain experience, however, we begin to become more concerned about our own professional growth and our effectiveness with a diverse population of students. We finally realize that becoming a good teacher means being a good learner.

- All teachers want to know how to maximize their teaching effectiveness.

In today's world, society and young people are changing so rapidly that it is critical to understand what our students are facing in order to determine appropriate instructional strategies. Today's students have grown up using technology in ways that many adults cannot even imagine. They have grown up with society and school violence. This new generation of learners demands a rejuvenation of teachers and perhaps a shift in the way we teach. These changes do not mean that we eliminate all the strategies that we have traditionally found effective. It simply means that we take a close look at what works for the growing diversity among kids. This change may mean reviving some of the traditional teaching approaches (we know what good teaching and learning look like); or in some cases, it may mean that we will have to stop using teaching strategies that aren't effective with students. As a very perceptive person once said, "When the horse dies, get off." Perhaps it is time for us to evaluate our current "horses" and see if any of them have died!

As teachers (especially for me as an English teacher), we have seen students who performed well on vocabulary tests one week and then two weeks (or two hours) later didn't even recognize the words in another context, let alone remember what they meant. No wonder so many of us get disappointed with the results of state tests (or ACT, SAT, AP, PSAT tests) when we have worked so hard and truly believed that our students had learned and understood the vocabulary we taught them. Unfortunately, many of our students are doing exactly what many of us did to get through school (if we will admit it); they are memorizing the words and definitions, putting them down on our tests to get a good grade or please the teacher, and then promptly forgetting them! The kids are making no connections to the words or even realizing how the words relate to learning in our content areas.

We cannot possibly teach every word that students don't know and understand in our classes, but we can and must teach our students ways to know and understand the critical vocabulary they need to be successful in school, ways to discover the meaning of any words they don't know, and ways to put that learning into long-term memory!

In *How To Teach Reading When You're Not a Reading Teacher* I examined ways that teachers could address the literacy needs of their students even if they didn't have a background in reading. I presented reading strategies that could be used in all content areas and at all grade levels, even though I focused on the middle level. In this book, I will elaborate only on vocabulary strategies because it has become apparent from research, daily practice, and standardized tests that if students do not know the "essential vocabulary" of the subjects they must take, they will not be successful in school or be able to show what they know and are able to do on standardized tests.

How to Teach Academic Vocabulary is intended to outline easy-to-use and practical vocabulary strategies for teachers who want to increase the academic achievement of all their students. I will begin with the research from best practice, literacy, and brain-based learning. I know that many educators often say, "Don't give me the research. Just tell me what to do in my classes." This always makes me sad because I believe that educators must be knowledgeable about why we do what we do. How else can we explain our teaching to a society that questions the quality of our work? If we don't know the research, how can we teach our students the best ways for them to know and remember things? With this idea in mind, I have strived to keep the research succinct and interesting. It is there for those of you who want to be consciously competent in your teaching and able to explain why you do what you do.

Good teachers often make their content come alive for students even if students can't read the text, but over the years I have come to believe that we are doing them a great disservice with this approach. If we value the content we are teaching (and we all love our own content), then we must give our students the strategies and skills they need to be self-sufficient learners when we're not there to provide information. We must help our students learn to value the content we love and we must give them a variety of ways to be successful without us.

This book is a compilation of the ideas and strategies collected from many sources and colleagues I have worked with over the years. I thank all of them for giving me valuable ideas that I could "borrow straight" or "borrow and adjust." Since there is no one "best way" to teach vocabulary (or anything else), tailor these techniques to your curriculum, your students, and your teaching style. Take the ones you like and make them work for you!

Sharon Faber

Chapter 1

The Research on Vocabulary

"Not only do students need a rich body of word knowledge to succeed in basic skill areas, they also need a specialized vocabulary to learn content area material."

– Baker, Simmons & Kameenui, 1995

What Do You Know About Effective Vocabulary Instruction?

Here is a list of 15 vocabulary instructional strategies. Based on your prior knowledge about teaching vocabulary, decide if each one is **effective** (E) or **ineffective** (I) as a way to enhance long-term memory and increase students' vocabulary in your content area. This is a preassessment so mark each one, even if you are not certain of the answer. By the time you finish this book, you will know the correct answers. Some of them may surprise you!

____ 1. Learning vocabulary words out of context or in isolation (for example, an ACT/SAT word list)

____ 2. Programmed vocabulary books or computer software

____ 3. Reading every day in every content area

____ 4. Playing and having fun with new words

____ 5. Using new vocabulary only when it is in the day's lesson

____ 6. Discussing antonyms and synonyms for new vocabulary

____ 7. Looking up definitions in a dictionary or glossary and writing a sentence using the new word

____ 8. Integrating new vocabulary into everyday language—reading, writing, and speaking

____ 9. Drill and practice involving multiple repetitions of the same type

___ 10. Teacher reading aloud when text is too difficult for students to read themselves or using an audiotape of the text

___ 11. Memorizing definitions

___ 12. Using graphic organizers or visuals to support new words—pictures, diagrams, charts

___ 13. Providing activities that integrate, repeat, and have meaningful use of new vocabulary words

___ 14. Explicit and systematic instruction of new vocabulary

___ 15. Multiple exposures to words in context

Why Do We Need to Know the Research?

As a consultant, I work with teachers and administrators all the time. It never fails to amaze me that I still get comments like, "Why do we need to look at research? Can't you just tell us what to do in our classes?" One of the problems educators face in today's society is the inability of many of us to explain why we do what we do. In a society where we are questioned about everything we do, and anyone who has been to school thinks he knows how we should teach and run schools, this inability becomes a liability. So, here is my list of reasons why educators need to know and understand the current research:

1. Research informs and confirms for educators what works best to help students learn and what instructional strategies teachers can use to help students.

2. Educators are *professionals*, as are doctors, dentists, accountants, and lawyers.

   Would you go to one of them who hadn't kept up on the latest research in their fields? If your answer is no, *then why should we expect parents to trust us if we're still doing what we've always been doing just because that's the way we do it?*

3. Educators need to be consciously competent and should be able to explain what they do and why they do it. Some teachers are unconsciously competent and do things that work without realizing exactly why they work or specifically what they have done. Learning does not happen by accident, and we should be able to explain why we do what we do in terms that lay people can understand.

   This is why many folks don't like research—it is usually written in a way that no one but researchers can understand!

4. Students in all classes deserve teachers who know how to best help them learn in an explicit and systematic way that will help them achieve to their best abilities.

5. If teachers know and understand the literacy, best practice, and brain research, it is never too late to help a student learn to read in any content!

   If you don't believe this part, then we might as well close up shop when students get to the fourth grade and beyond and can't do reading or math at the level that we expect.

Now that you know my philosophy about our need to be informed professionals and have completed your preassessment, let's look at what the research tells us about vocabulary instruction.

What Does the Research Say and What Does That Mean?

Teachers know that there are student factors outside of school, like home life and childhood experiences, that have a big influence on student success in school. We also know that we can't change those factors, but they do make the "playing field" at school uneven. Students from disadvantaged homes come to school lacking in background knowledge about life and school as well as the specific vocabulary needed to be successful in a school setting. They've had many types of experiences and know many words, but they are most likely not the experiences or words that will make them successful at school. Some kids come to school *reading ready*, and others don't even know to hold their books right side up or that their eyes go left to right across the page when they read. Some kids have been on vacations and have parents that read to them, and still other kids have never been outside their own communities. Without background knowledge and vocabulary, many students have problems with reading comprehension, writing, and communicating in their content specific classes. Classes like history, science, career and technical education courses, and even reading and English use unfamiliar words that many students cannot understand; and if students can't understand the words, they can't comprehend when they read.

We often expect our students to know the words they need to be successful in our classes because they have been exposed to them in earlier grades. In fact, if you examine the verbs in your state standards by grade level, you will see that many of the verbs are exactly the same year after year for what we want students to know and be able to do. Why is it then that many students move right up the grades and never understand what it means to compare and contrast, infer, or summarize? Unfortunately, too many of our students have "word poverty," and this lack of academic vocabulary will widen the gap that exists between successful and unsuccessful students in today's high-stakes, standards-based educational environment. We must equip our students to be successful in academic contexts. Lack of vocabulary knowledge is a serious obstacle for many of our students, impacting not only their reading, but also their writing and communicating. One of the primary responsibilities of teachers at all grade levels is to provide opportunities for students to enlarge their listening, speaking, reading, and writing vocabularies.

My favorite resource for reading research is *Put Reading First: The Research Building Blocks for Teaching Children to Read* (PRF) which first came out in 2001 from the National Institute for Literacy (NIFL).

As I write this book, Put Reading First *is in its third edition, and while the cover says it is for Kindergarten through Grade 3, I believe it is critical for all teachers, regardless of the grade levels they teach, to read it. This important research went out from the federal government to every elementary school in this country; however, many folks didn't read it or realize its importance. From my point of view as a nonresearcher, it is written like good research should be written.*

It has pictures, it uses great colors to guide the reader to important points, and the language is easy to understand so that "normal" people can read and use it. It is a compilation of over 30 years of research from the National Reading Panel (NRP) report in 2000 on how to successfully teach children to read. Each chapter on the five elements of reading

> "Vocabulary refers to words that we must know to communicate effectively."
> (PRF, p. 29)

(phonemic awareness, phonics, fluency, vocabulary, and comprehension) defines the skill, reviews the research evidence, gives implications for classroom instruction, describes proven strategies, and even gives frequently asked questions with the answers! What more could a teacher want?

Since the focus of this book is the importance of academic vocabulary and how we must teach it so kids can remember key words "forever," I want to start with what the *Put Reading First (PRF)* resource and other research tell us about the critical role of vocabulary in the two stages of reading development: **learning to read—Pre-K through grade 3** and **reading to learn—grades 4 through 12 and beyond**.

Vocabulary Development:

There are four kinds of vocabulary that we must know to be able to communicate in life or in any content area in school.

1. **Listening**—*the words we need to know to understand what we hear*

   If you think about it, your listening vocabulary is the largest vocabulary that you have and it comes first in life. Even babies and pets have a listening vocabulary and know many words before they ever learn to speak. They communicate in nonverbal ways with those words by gestures and reactions to words they hear. Do you have a pet that reacts immediately to words like *potty*, *walk*, or *treat*? My dog would start jumping and prancing every time we said *walk*. We started spelling the word, so she wouldn't get excited. Over time, she started reacting when she heard *w-a-l-k*. Young kids do the same thing as their listening vocabularies grow. How many parents have spelled *cookie* and been amazed when their child started screaming?

2. **Speaking**—*the words we use when we speak*

Your speaking vocabulary comes next in life, but it is not as large as your listening vocabulary. Both kids and adults recognize many words they hear spoken, but they do not use all words as part of their speaking vocabularies. We all recognize some big words like *conundrum*, *epiphany*, *philanthropy*, *photosynthesis*, *oxymoron*, and *odyssey* when we hear them, but we don't use them when we speak because we are unsure of their correct use.

3. **Reading**—*the words we need to know to understand what we read*

Reading is the vocabulary we develop as we transfer our listening and speaking vocabularies to recognizing the printed words on a page. If English were an easy language, this step would not be difficult; however, the English language is very difficult and has too many words that don't look like they sound on paper. For example, think about the word *antique*. Many students would pronounce this word *an-ti-que* when they saw it in print. If you read it the way it looks, you may not have word recognition based on your listening and speaking vocabularies. The same holds true for many words such as *bosom* and *segue*. Many adults fail to say those words correctly when they see them in print! A reading vocabulary is a big jump from the listening and speaking vocabularies that kids bring to school. Readers must recognize the word and know what the majority of words in a sentence mean, before they can understand what they are reading (PRF, p. 39).

4. **Writing**—*the words we use in writing*

Writing vocabularies are the smallest and hardest to develop. Even though we may know many words, using them correctly in writing is not easy.

I bet many of you went through college as I did, writing papers and then using a Thesaurus to put big words in place of the little ones that you had used!

Levels of Word Knowledge

There are three levels of vocabulary comprehension; that is, students know words in varying degrees. If students are to understand the text they read in their classes, teachers must know these levels and be able to scaffold vocabulary instruction to link academic vocabulary to their students' prior knowledge.

- **Established**

  Students know the word easily and rapidly. It is part of their prior knowledge and can be used to begin building on new word recognition (*trip*).

- **Acquainted**

  Students recognize the word and understand the basic meaning. The word is partially understood, but clarification is needed (*journey*).

- **Unknown Words**

  The students encounter a new word and the meaning is not known. Though it is not in their oral or reading vocabulary, the new word represents known concepts (*expedition*).

Isabel Beck et. al. (2002) further characterize word knowledge into three basic categories: Tier 1, Tier 2, or Tier 3. Words in Tier 3 are the focus of this book, because they represent academic vocabulary.

- Tier 1—**Established** or known words

  This tier includes most basic words. They rarely require instruction. Students know the words easily and rapidly (prior knowledge), and the words can be used to begin building recognitions of new words (*trip, clock, baby, happy, walk, outside*).

- Tier 2—**Acquainted** words

  This tier represents words of high frequency for mature language users. Students recognize these words and understand their basic meaning, but clarification is needed (*journey, avoid, inspect, sensible, grateful*).

- Tier 3—**Unknown** words (academic vocabulary)

  This tier has words with content-specific meaning. These new words are rarely used and their meaning is unknown. The words are not in the oral or reading vocabulary of students, but represent known concepts (*expedition, isotope, latitude, photosynthesis, condiment*).

How to Teach Academic Vocabulary

According to David Sousa (2005), the scientific research says that some vocabulary must be taught directly but that most vocabulary is learned indirectly. He states that the research has shown the following:

- Children learn the meanings of most words indirectly through everyday experience with oral and written language when they have conversations with others, listen to adults read to them, and read on their own.

- Children learn vocabulary words directly when they are explicitly taught individual words and word-learning strategies.

- Direct instruction is most effective for teaching difficult words representing complex concepts that are not part of the children's everyday experiences.

- Repeated exposure to vocabulary in many contexts helps word learning. The more children see, hear, and read specific words, the better they learn them and their various meanings.

Factors like ability, age, and text density have an effect on vocabulary acquisition (Swanborn and de Glopper, 1999). Text density measures the number of new words in a given number of words. The lower the text density (for example, one new word in 150 words), the greater the chances of learning that new word (30 percent). The chances drop to only seven percent when the text density reaches one new word in ten words.

What We Know About Vocabulary Acquisition

Here are some of the conclusions researchers have drawn:

- By the time good readers reach high school, they have approximately 1,000,000 words in their four vocabularies, whereas struggling readers may have only 100,000 words (Nagy & Anderson, 1984).

- By 12th grade, high-performing students know approximately four times as many words as their low-performing peers (Graves, Brunetti & Slater, 1982).

- For a high school student who takes five subjects a day, learning ten new words every day in each subject would result in as many as 1,800 new words per school year (in addition to those learned from other content reading) (Nagy, Anderson & Herman, 1987).

- Approximately 30 root words, prefixes, and suffixes provide the basis for more than 14,000 commonly used words in the English language (Brown & Cazden, 1965).

- Older students learn words better when they are connected together in meaningful phrases rather than presented as single words (Rasinski, 1990).

- To increase content knowledge, students must learn how words they already know are used in the content area. According to Searls and Klesius (1984), there are at least 99 common words in English with four or more different definitions or applications.

- Vocabulary acquisition is crucial to academic development. Not only do students need a rich body of word knowledge to succeed in basic skill areas, they also need a specialized vocabulary to learn content area material (Baker, Simmons & Kameenui, 1995).

- **All teachers must teach vocabulary directly through their content!**

How Can We Translate Vocabulary Research into Practice?

Vocabulary is important to reading comprehension, and comprehension is the biggest problem most teachers from grades 2 through 12 experience. We have many students who can *read* the words, but have no clue about what they are reading. Students must understand what most of the words mean when they read or they will not be able to learn the content. Too often when we teach vocabulary in schools, it is boring and requires little thinking. How exciting is it for students to write a word, look it up in the dictionary, choose the shortest or first definition, write a sentence using the word, and then take a test (usually matching or multiple choice questions)?

> *"Very few older struggling readers need help to read the words on a page; their most common problem is that they are not able to comprehend what they read."*
>
> *(Reading Next, p. 3)*

Students develop knowledge about a word gradually as they have repeated exposure to it. They move from not knowing the word at all to recognizing that they have seen or heard the word before. Once the word is somewhat familiar, they develop partial knowledge, in which they have a general sense of what the word means, or they know at least one meaning for the word. When students have full word knowledge, they know multiple meanings and can use the word in a variety of ways. Teachers can help students learn new content-specific academic vocabulary through direct, explicit instruction.

If we are going to change our approach to teaching vocabulary so that academic words can really be understood and used by students, teachers are going to have to use exciting and engaging vocabulary instruction that is research-based and practical. We are going to have to help students develop an interest and awareness in words beyond vocabulary in school assignments. Teachers at every grade level and in every content area are going to have to help students notice words in real-life situations and then help them explore relationships among words from school and life. Think of these as guidelines for teaching academic vocabulary:

- **Limit the number of words we teach at one time and concentrate on key concepts.**

  The vocabulary and concepts must be taught in semantically related clusters so students can see the relationships among them.

- **Model how to determine a word's meaning in text material by thinking aloud.**

  When teachers share their thinking process, they are demonstrating a strategy for students to use. Encourage students to imitate this process. After all, teachers are the experts!

- **Teach students how to use dictionaries and glossaries appropriately** so they can be used as sources to figure out what new words mean.

- **Choose strategies that will help students learn the critical vocabulary and concepts and their relationships to each other** (roots, affixes, definition, example, illustration, contrast, logic, etc.).

- **Make word study active and engaging** so students can understand words well enough to be able to use them appropriately during their everyday lives.

Chapter 2

What Is Academic Vocabulary?

"Background knowledge manifests itself as vocabulary knowledge. Words are labels for our knowledge packets; the more words we have, the more packets of knowledge, the more background knowledge."

– Robert Marzano, 2004

Everybody Talks About It, But What Is It Really?

Start with these important premises:

- Academic vocabulary is the language of school and the language of print in texts.

- Academic vocabulary is the language that students need to know in order to be successful in each content area.

- Without instruction in academic vocabulary, many students will not learn the content.

- Many students have oral academic vocabulary skills and can get the gist of their texts without really understanding the academic vocabulary or being able to critically read and understand them.

- Academic vocabulary entails four language skills: speaking, listening, reading, and writing. The most challenging are reading and writing.

- Students with high-poverty backgrounds arrive at school with fewer experiences than students from economically advantaged homes. A limited set of experiences can mean limited academic vocabulary and concepts.

The Rationale for Teaching Vocabulary Strategies in All Subject Areas and at All Grade Levels

> *"Vocabulary knowledge in kindergarten and first grade is a significant predictor of reading comprehension in the middle and secondary grades."*
> *– Cunningham & Stanovich, 2005*

> *"Teaching vocabulary can improve reading comprehension for both native English speakers and English-language learners."*
> *– Carlo et al., 2004*

Learning vocabulary is a huge task and it is essential for life and school success. Many children, especially children of poverty and English language learners, enter school with vocabulary deficits and with vocabularies much smaller than their middle-class, native-English speaking counterparts. Once in school, these children continue to learn words at about half the rate of their peers, and this increasing gap puts them at severe risk of failing school (Chall & Jacobs, 2003; Hart & Risley, 2003).

The original vocabulary deficit of these kids along with the learning gap that follows in school creates a problem with learning academic vocabulary. Without knowledge of academic vocabulary, students are at a loss and a great disadvantage when they have to learn what schools and teachers want them to know. I have found over the years that as students go through school, most teachers expect them to remember what they learned the year before. While this doesn't seem to be a bad idea (or really even asking too much of our students), the problem is that most students are not able to build on that previous learning unless a really good teacher did something in a way that made the content memorable. With that thought in mind, I believe that there are six things that all teachers must do in their classrooms if we want students not only to learn, but also to remember what we teach them, especially academic vocabulary.

1. **Create a receptive state for student learning that is risk free.**

   In other words, teachers need to do their best to make students like them and their subject.

   Now, I've had folks tell me that they didn't go into teaching to be popular. They just want to get kids to learn. Well, they are naïve (or dumb) because all teachers had better understand that if kids like you, they will learn from you. We don't need to be their friends, but we sure had better be adult advocates who believe that students can and will learn, if we do our jobs successfully and provide them with the appropriate opportunities to learn.

2. **Make content meaningful to students' lives.**

   I don't want to hurt anyone's feelings, but have you noticed that a lot of what we teach in school is difficult for students to relate to in their lives? If we tell them they need it for the test or for the next year's teacher, they don't see the value. By the way, have you noticed that teachers don't listen to announcements or read memos that are not focused on their content, grade level, and so on? It's human nature to be attentive to what is important to you and to be uninterested when it doesn't relate to you. Kids feel the same way.

3. Get and maintain students' attention.

I hate to say it, but a lot of what we teach in schools is boring. Teachers have favorite subjects, even if they teach all of them. I didn't know how true this was until I became an administrator and had to observe all the teachers in my building. I would find myself trying to stay alert in some of the classes and I felt sorry that kids had to go through that every day. Don't you ever remember a teacher who was boring and didn't hold your attention or a subject that you just couldn't get excited about?

4. Help students retain information.

This is the key to being a great teacher. We must use the brain research, best practice research, and the literacy research so we will know how our students learn best and what we can do to help them learn. We must also understand the characteristics of the age group we teach so that our choice of instructional strategies is developmentally appropriate.

5. Help students transfer learning.

We need to help our students make connections among all the subjects and content areas that they encounter in school. While teachers realize that we all teach very similar skills like questioning, predicting, summarizing, and comparing and contrasting, the students don't make those connections unless teachers tell them that predicting in English or social studies is like estimating in math or hypothesizing in science. Does it bother you that many students can do half notes, quarter notes, and full notes in music, but they can't do fractions in math? We must help them make connections so they can transfer learning to new situations—like state tests.

6. Teach direct, explicit learning strategies in a systematic way.

This is probably the most important thing that great teachers do in their classrooms. They understand that their students do not automatically transfer skills they learn in reading classes or other classes to their content areas. Great teachers are the experts in their content areas and can identify key concepts, critical vocabulary, text features, and reading-thinking skills that are needed to learn in their content. They know how to model the skills their students need to use and learn for success. In fact, great teachers create enthusiasm for their subjects. Reading comprehension is basic to learning in every content area, so great teachers accept the responsibility of helping students learn to use learning strategies, activities, and games to understand specific content vocabulary.

What Does a Vocabulary-Conscious Classroom Look Like?

> *"People with large vocabularies tend to be intrigued by words and enjoy playing with them."*
> (Beck, McKeown & Kucan, 2002)

If teachers follow the previous six suggestions, then their classrooms are focused on learning and the needs of students. Not only that, but their classrooms are probably places where academic vocabulary is part of daily learning. If you have made your classroom "vocabulary conscious," you will see the following things happening:

• Students' reading and writing is valued and celebrated.

• A variety of reading and writing experiences are available.

• Students read and write—every day.

• Teachers read aloud—every day.

• There is a lot of content word play.

• There is joy and laughter in the learning of the content

Michael Graves also described a vocabulary-conscious classroom in his book *The Vocabulary Book*, 2006. His definition goes right along with what I believe we should see in great teachers' classrooms. He says that in a vocabulary-conscious classroom, teachers include four things:

• **Rich and Varied Language Experiences**
Independent reading, reading aloud, exposure to oral language (speaking, listening, discussing), writing.

• **The Teaching of Individual Words**
Instruction in select words found in texts read independently or during read-aloud times, and words to be used in writing.

• **The Teaching of Word-Learning Strategies**
Teaching structural analysis (roots, affixes, Latin and Greek cognates), contextual analysis, and the use of tools (dictionary and thesaurus).

• **The Promoting of Word Consciousness**
Word and language play, figurative language, and developing metacognitive knowledge with regard to words.

What Is Academic Vocabulary?

According to most sources, there are two kinds of academic vocabulary that teachers and students must work with in school.

General Academic Vocabulary

First, there are *general academic words*. These are the terms that are useful for, but not critical to, understanding the concepts of content. They are more formal than the Tier 1 or established words that are known to most students, although they are rarely used in everyday conversation. "Stop" is a common Tier 1 expression, while "conclude" is a similar but more formal word, a general academic term that would be used in a school setting. Some words that teachers often use and assume students understand when they teach are also general academic vocabulary because they are more formal. These more formal and mature words are often considered Tier 2 words. Good examples of these words would be *however* and *therefore*. Both words show relationships and connections and are often found in textbooks (and in teachers' lectures or lessons), but they are not used in general conversation. Teachers across all content areas should agree on these general academic terms, so they can be practiced and reinforced for students.

Content-Specific Academic Vocabulary

The second kind of academic vocabulary is easier for teachers and students to recognize, but not necessarily easier for teachers to teach or students to learn. These are the *content-specific words* or Tier 3—terms that are critical and often unknown. When students understand content-specific words, they are more likely to understand the content. Think about terms like *blog, Twitter, megapixel,* and *Facebook* that are related to technology. Most of us had to learn those content-specific terms by actually experiencing them and not just reading about them. If you understand those terms, someone probably guided you through a specific task. Students, especially English language learners, need this same kind of instruction. They need to experience content-specific academic vocabulary in a meaningful way through systematic and explicit instruction.

According to Marzano (2005) the strongest action a teacher can take to ensure that students have the academic background knowledge to understand the content they will encounter is providing them with direct instruction in these terms. When students understand the terms, it is easier for them to understand the information they will read and hear in class.

Traditional Vocabulary Practices That Don't Always Work to Teach Academic Vocabulary

There are several commonly used practices for presenting and learning academic vocabulary that are not always effective.

1. Looking up words in the dictionary or glossary

One of the most used vocabulary strategies is for teachers to give kids a list of important words for a unit of study (usually on Monday), tell them to look the words up in the dictionary or glossary, and then to write their own sentences using the words. The plan is to go over the words and sentences (usually on Wednesday), so they can be ready to read the material better and take a vocabulary test (usually on Friday). As most teachers know, this plan doesn't work too well; dictionaries and glossaries use definitions that are precise and concise, and many words have multiple meanings to choose from. Kids often choose either the first or shortest definition. In fact, sometimes the definitions are harder to understand than the original word! What kids need are definitions that are in familiar language that they can understand and an age-appropriate example that is relevant to their own experiences. This is why good teachers scaffold vocabulary instruction and give kid-friendly definitions and then relate the new word to words that students already know. Looking up a word doesn't help understanding or long-term recall because it isolates the learning of vocabulary from the subject matter. Just defining words is not enough to understand concepts. Students need word-learning strategies that can help them learn what new concepts mean, as well as see the connections between these concepts.

I don't want anyone to think that using external references to help students understand words is not good. In fact, using textbook aids like glossaries, dictionaries, and indexes can be very helpful to students at a certain point in their learning of academic vocabulary. These resources just shouldn't be the first strategy we use to teach new vocabulary. They are more valuable for long-term memory once students have an initial understanding, background knowledge, and experience with the new terms. However, I must warn you that we often think students know how to use these resources when they don't!

If you want your students to use textbook aids to help figure out unknown words, take the time to show them how to use the aids. This includes the glossary, index, or dictionary. Many kids don't know about guide words, how to use the pronunciation key, or how to choose the best definition. For those who want to use the Internet, teach students how to use: www.onelook.com, www.alphadictionary.com, www.yourdictionary.com, www.usingenglish.com, www.dictionary.com.

2. Using context clues to figure out word meanings

This strategy sounds like a great thing to do to help kids understand what they are reading, but what if you have a student with limited experience in the content or one who is a struggling reader? Consider how a struggling student would feel if the only words he recognized around the new word were *a*, *and*, and *the*. These words certainly are not helpful in figuring out a science term like photosynthesis. While some students can figure out new vocabulary through incidental learning from context, research indicates that the odds of figuring out the intended meaning of an unknown word from written context is extremely low (varying from 5 percent to 15 percent for both native speakers and English-language learners) (Beck et al. 2002; Nagy et al. 1985). This is why good teachers once again scaffold instruction and teach kids the word skills they need to figure out content-specific vocabulary.

I don't want you to think that context clues are all bad. (A lot of us use them all the time when we read, but we've got degrees and the teachers' guides to help us—our students don't.) It is possible to help students by modeling and thinking aloud about what you do when you figure out new words by using context clues. (Now remember, just telling students to figure out the word by using the words around it won't always work because many textbooks are not reader friendly and do not help with appropriate context clues.) You'll need to analyze your text and see how it is organized in order to know how to help students use it effectively. If you're going to teach context clues, you need to teach students the signal words found in a text. There are three kinds of context clues that you can use to help students: definitions, descriptions, and compare and contrast.

- **Definition** works in some textbooks because new words or concepts may be underlined or in bold and then they give the definition in the same sentence. The problem is that publishers may not always select the same words that teachers think are important to know for long-term memory.

- **Description** is another way that some text helps readers understand new words or ideas. The word is described in the text in a way that the reader can make a good guess at its meaning. You'll need to model what a good description looks like in your text a number of times for students so that they understand what they are looking for.

- **Compare and Contrast** is used in texts where the new word or idea is compared with another word or idea to show something similar or to illustrate something that is the opposite. Once again, the teacher must recognize this approach and show students what to look for.

3. **Depending on unplanned "teachable moments"**

All teachers know that we don't always realize which words our students know and don't know until one of them asks a question and we have the opportunity to expand on the unknown words. We are often surprised at which words our kids don't know until one of these teachable moments occurs. While these extemporaneous vocabulary teaching moments are wonderful and deepen student understanding, good teachers know that they must analyze the text and determine which content-specific words are critical to comprehension and then consciously plan how to teach those terms if our students are going to be successful in our content.

Just because a word is in a book and the student doesn't know it, doesn't mean that we have to teach every unknown word. That would take us forever! Think about all the padding that many textbooks put in that does not have to be learned to understand the content.

Remember when you were in college—how many times did you highlight almost every single line on a page because it was new information and you didn't know it? Students don't have to know everything in a book!

What Does Work to Teach Academic Vocabulary?

If we know what doesn't work as we teach academic vocabulary, what does work? Well, there are many strategies, activities, and games that teachers can use to increase academic vocabulary for their students, but there are four major categories of instructional approaches you can consciously incorporate into your classroom to help students learn and remember more of the important information that we want them to know. These four categories will not be a surprise to most teachers.

1. Increase the amount of reading

This is the most difficult thing for a teacher to get students to do. If we can't get them to read the material the first time, how are we going to get them to read it again or even to read other information about the same topic? Well, the answer is to trick them into reading (good teachers are sly . . .) by teaching them specific strategies that great readers in your content (scientists, literature specialists, auto mechanics, mathematicians, chefs, historians) use when they read to understand new words and content. Teachers must consciously plan and design tasks that will increase vocabulary learning through reading practice.

I have used a variety of tricks to get my students to read more over the years, so I'll share a few with you. Some teachers feel uncomfortable about using this approach, but my theory is use whatever works to get kids to do something that I want done because they want to do it. I always begin the year with a textbook walk and very carefully teach the kids how to use their text. I go over all text features first, and then I do a chapter walk using the first chapter as a think aloud to help them realize some of the "tricks" that good readers use to get the most out of their reading. Many students, usually the struggling ones, see these tricks as cheating so they love it! I've had students who never read anything before they got to my class start reading because they thought they were getting away with something. I'm always amazed that they don't know simple things like:

- **Always read the introduction and conclusion of the chapter first.** These sections give you the main things that you need to know, and you can have the general idea of what the chapter is going to be about in case you run out of time for reading the rest of the chapter.

- **Always read the questions at the end of the chapter before you start reading** so you'll know what to read for and won't spend time learning things you don't need to know.

- **Whenever you have to read a paragraph and figure out the main idea, read the first and last sentence first.** Most of the time, this will give you what you need to know.

I think you get the idea, and I know that you'll come up with some great "tricks" that will help students in your content. What you're doing with this type of approach is helping kids become good consumers of the learning in your classroom and leveling the playing field for students who don't do these kinds of things innately.

2. Use systematic and explicit "direct" vocabulary instruction

Routine and consistency in teaching vocabulary can be a very effective and efficient way to teach students new words that they can put in long-term memory. It is not enough to say that we preview, introduce, cover, or review new terms. There are specific steps that will help students retain content vocabulary, and teachers need to use them. Students learn more words through targeted instruction than they do just through independent reading, where they often gain only superficial understanding of many words or they develop misconceptions about those words that interfere with their understanding of what the words really mean.

If we expect teachers to use systematic and explicit instruction, we had better define what the terms are so we will all understand them in the same way. (Consider these two terms the academic vocabulary necessary to understand this book.) So, what is systematic instruction? When a teacher systematically teaches, the skills and concepts are taught in a planned, logically progressive sequence that can be repeated; it then becomes well understood by students because they recognize it when the teacher is consistent and uses the process. What is explicit instruction? Explicit instruction is direct instruction and includes the following steps:

How to Teach Academic Vocabulary
©Copyright Incentive Publications, Inc., Nashville, TN

- Direct explanation by the teacher
  in student-friendly terms or experiences
- Teacher modeling
- Guided practice
- Independent practice
- Application

3. Teach word-learning strategies

Students can independently learn new words when they learn to use vocabulary strategies from the content teachers. The teachers model the strategies and guide students through them until they are part of their learning routines (systematic and explicit instruction).

Strategies like analyzing the parts of words (roots, prefixes, suffixes), using graphic organizers, and developing acronyms are some of the techniques that can be used to increase students' abilities to learn and then store in long-term memory challenging academic vocabulary. It may surprise you to know that approximately 80 percent of the words in an English dictionary contain Greek and Latin roots and affixes. The four major prefixes un-, re-, dis-, in- (im-, ir-) account for 58 percent of prefixed words read in school materials in upper grades, and 87 percent of prefixed words also have suffixes. Of those words with suffixes, 62 percent are the inflectional suffixes -s, -es, -ed, -ing, and about 27 percent have the derivational suffixes -able, -ible, -ness, -ly (White, Powers, White, 1989). Students should be taught to apply their knowledge of word parts to the new words they find in their textbooks, so they can form generalizations through informed guessing and make predictions about the new words' meanings.

4. Create word-conscious classrooms

Vocabulary develops when teachers create a word-rich environment and students engage in various activities to increase language play, word choice in writing, sensitivity to word parts, and understanding of word originations. Students need to understand that new words may be synonyms for words they already know and that there are some known words that have multiple meanings. They already know from being in school that some of the words or concepts used in most content classes are totally new to them. Students need to see learning academic vocabulary as a fun and challenging activity, not drudgery! Word-conscious classrooms integrate metacognition about words, motivate students to learn words, and create deep and lasting interest in words. Fostering word consciousness differs from grade to grade and content to content, but it is important in every classroom. There are some time-consuming, word-consciousness activities, but for the most part, it does not take a lot of time for the teacher or the student (Grave & Watts-Taffe, 2007).

Puns and having fun with words is one way I love to create a word-conscious classroom. A good resource for content puns is *Get Thee to a Punnery* by Richard Lederer. Another one of my favorites to use with kids (and adults) of all ages is the *Weighty Word Book* by Levitt, Burger, and Guralnick. Both are great books that show how to enjoy and explore words as you really learn them in a memorable way. There are many other so-called "kid" books that are a pleasure to use with older students because they teach abstract concepts in a very concrete way, in terms that all students can understand.

I put a list of some good ones at the end of the book in case you want to try them. I know there are many more available, so talk to your librarian or media specialists to get other ideas.

Just for Fun: Puns For The Intelligent . . .

1. The roundest knight at King Arthur's round table was Sir Cumference. He acquired his size from too much pi.

2. I thought I saw an eye doctor on an Alaskan island, but it turned out to be an optical Aleutian.

3. She was only a whisky maker, but he loved her still.

4. A rubber-band pistol was confiscated from algebra class because it was a weapon of math disruption.

5. The butcher backed into the meat grinder and got a little behind in his work.

6. No matter how much you push the envelope, it'll still be stationery.

7. A dog gave birth to puppies near the road and was cited for littering.

8. A grenade thrown into a kitchen in France would result in Linoleum Blownapart.

9. Two silkworms had a race. They ended up in a tie.

10. Time flies like an arrow. Fruit flies like a banana.

11. Two antennas met on a roof, fell in love, and got married. The ceremony wasn't much, but the reception was excellent.

12. Two peanuts walk into a bar and one was a salted.

13. Two cannibals are eating a clown. One says to the other, "Does this taste funny to you?"

14. An invisible man marries an invisible woman. The kids were nothing to look at, either.

15. I went to buy some camouflage trousers the other day but I didn't see any.

16. I went to a seafood disco last week and pulled a mussel.

17. Two men sitting in a kayak were chilly so they lit a fire in the boat. Not surprisingly, it sank, proving once again that you can't have your kayak and heat it, too.

18. Don't join dangerous cults; practice safe sects.

19. In democracy, it's your vote that counts. In feudalism, it's your count that votes.

20. A chicken crossing the road is poultry in motion.

How to Teach Academic Vocabulary

How Do I Teach Academic Vocabulary in My Classroom?

Many students can comprehend orally but may struggle when they read text independently. In Chapter 3 you will find specific strategies, activities, and games to use to teach academic vocabulary effectively in any content area but here is a general list of things that many teachers do in their classrooms. Think about which ones you already do and which ones you want to focus on developing.

1. Have students read a variety of fiction and nonfiction texts. Extensive reading is the most powerful way to develop reading comprehension.
   - Wide reading increases the number of words that students automatically recognize.
   - Wide reading improves syntactic competence.

2. Do read-alouds of text that is too difficult for students to read.

3. Use listening stations where students listen to audio tapes and follow along with text that is too difficult for them to read independently.

4. Integrate new vocabulary into everyday language—speaking, reading, and writing.

5. Model and use new vocabulary on a regular basis with students.

6. Create a language-rich, word-conscious classroom.

7. Play with and have fun with new words.

8. Plan multiple, meaningful exposures to words in context.

9. Support vocabulary instruction with visuals appropriate to their content (pictures, diagrams, graphic organizers, graphs, and charts).

10. Extend the depth of student understanding about new vocabulary—scaffold the learning.

11. Analyze word structure—syllables, affixes, roots, and base.

12. Discuss antonyms, synonyms, examples, and nonexamples for new vocabulary.

13. Provide activities that ensure integration, repetition, and meaningful use of new vocabulary words.

14. **Provide explicit and systematic instruction in how to independently learn new vocabulary.**

Final Thoughts on the Importance of Academic Vocabulary

Every teacher—at every grade level and in all content areas—needs to focus on vocabulary instruction because understanding vocabulary improves comprehension. Each content area has its own unique vocabulary, terminology, and language, particularly the labels used to identify important content-area concepts. Content-area vocabulary terms need to be systematically and explicitly taught because they are rarely part of the concepts that students already know. Students have no prior knowledge with which

> *"In a successful vocabulary program, words do not appear as part of a classroom exercise and then drop from sight."*
>
> – Beck

to connect the terms, although the terms are often semantically related. If one science or math term is understood, others may be connected and understood. Since a lack of experience can become a barrier to learning new concepts or ideas, teachers need to find creative ways to help students develop and expand their knowledge base through direct exposure, discussion, analogies, and explanations for content-area concepts. Content-area teachers need to provide students a variety of opportunities to work with and experience these concepts in context and to explore relationships among them.

> *"Vocabulary knowledge is a crucial factor underlying reading comprehension and thinking more generally."*
>
> – (Stahl & Stahl, 2004)

> *"The teacher who is alert to opportunities for using sophisticated, interesting, and precise language is probably the most important element in a verbal-rich environment."*
>
> – Beck

Chapter 3

A Nifty Fifty—Vocabulary Strategies, Activities, and Games

"Effective teachers intentionally focus on enriching and expanding students' vocabulary knowledge and model inquisitiveness about words and their meanings; they also help students develop their own skills as independent word learners."

– Nagy & Scott, 2000

Figuring out how to get kids to learn and then remember the vocabulary necessary to be successful in school is not an easy task. If it were, our classrooms would be filled with successful students who understood everything they read. Too often we don't address the importance of knowing specific words that help us understand what we read and hear in content-area classes. We know our students don't understand what they're reading and that their comprehension is weak. We ignore the fact that, without excellent vocabulary learning strategies reinforced by vocabulary activities and games, many of our students will not progress as fast as they could, and others will not access the content at all.

Many purposeful vocabulary strategies are readily available for teachers and students. This chapter is a collection of fifty strategies, activities, and games that will help a diverse range of students learn academic vocabulary in a systematic and explicit way. They are compatible with what research tells us about how the brain learns and are designed to help students retain academic vocabulary in long-term memory. The *Nifty Fifty* ideas are effective in any content area or grade level, and most are easy for teachers to incorporate into lessons without changing much of what they already do.

What Do We Know about Instructional Strategies?

Vocabulary research provides this wisdom about instructional strategies for vocabulary:

- Some strategies adapt or work better in different curricular areas than others.

- Every student will not relate to each and every strategy.

- Whatever the students' reading level or ability to comprehend text might be, it is the teacher's responsibility to make the textbook material accessible and meaningful to them.

- To get the greatest benefit out of any strategy, begin by modeling it for your students—use the strategy yourself and "think aloud" as you go through the steps *(metacognition)*.

- A strategy is effective when you begin with something that is familiar and easily understood so students can quickly reach a comfort level with the activity before attempting it with more difficult materials *(scaffolding)*.

As you add to your repertoire of vocabulary-acquisition strategies, activities, and games, be selective about what you choose for your classes. Just as students can't be expected to know every unknown word in their textbooks, you can't be expected to use every strategy, activity, and game that you find in this book. Begin by choosing the ones that are comfortable for you. As you decide what to choose, keep these questions in mind.

1. Which strategies, activities, and games ignite enthusiasm for you? Which ones can you use to build content-area language?

2. Which strategies, activities, and games will help students relate the new vocabulary words to experiences and concepts that they already know? *(students' prior knowledge)*

3. Which strategies, activities, and games will limit the number of words taught in each unit so you can concentrate on key concepts?

4. Which strategies, activities, and games will help you teach terms and concepts in semantically related clusters so that students can clearly see the associations among related terms and concepts?

5. Which strategies and activities model graphic organizers for students? Can you allow students enough practice in working with the strategies and activities, as well as the graphic organizers, so that their use becomes a habit?

6. Which strategies and activities can you repeatedly model in lessons to determine a word's meaning so that students can observe you and know what to do when they encounter unfamiliar words and you are not there to help them?

7. Which strategies, activities, and games do you find most useful as a content specialist? Which strategies would you choose to use yourself if you were learning new information in your content (in a college class)?

How to Teach Academic Vocabulary

What Elements Best Engage Students in Vocabulary Experiences?

Remember, in order for students to put new understandings into long-term memory, there must be active, engaged learning. The two most powerful ways to engage students are to use **visualization** and **hands-on activities**. The way I like to meet both requirements for active learning is to incorporate foldables and graphic organizers. These hands-on activities require students to manipulate the content and use visualization. They take very little time to make and are student friendly. (They're teacher friendly too, because the kids do all the cutting and folding!)

Foldables and **flipbooks** are easy ways to use a sheet of paper creatively so that students have something visual and concrete to help them put ideas into long-term memory. *It is hard for me to separate the two because when you use foldables, they often become flipbooks.* If you think about it, students have always used foldables (making paper airplanes to throw at other students during class or intricate thumb boxes to unfold in a variety of shapes to entertain themselves while we were teaching), but now teachers have actually given the different folds names to incorporate "folding paper" into teaching. You can fold paper in a variety of ways—a hamburger fold, a hot-dog fold, a taco fold, and many more.

Graphic organizers have been used for a long time as a teaching tool. A graphic organizer is a visual aid that helps define hierarchical relationships among concepts. It lends itself particularly well to the teaching of technical vocabulary (Dunston, 1992; Moore & Readence, 1984). Academic vocabulary is very technical, so it is no surprise that most vocabulary strategies and activities use graphic organizers to help students analyze the content, determine the most significant concepts, and classify critical information. However, graphic organizers (like any other good teaching tool) must be used purposefully.

Graphic organizers can be used before, during, and after reading to increase comprehension. They help students understand and retain information by organizing abstract terms and concepts into a format connected to information they already know. Begin by deciding which graphic organizer is best suited to what you are teaching and teach it to your students. Remember the discussion in Chapter 2 about focusing on several strategies and learning them well before teaching new strategies? That principle applies here. Use a few organizers (the ones that you feel best fit your content area) until your students are able to use them with success independently. Your goal is to move to a point where students are able to analyze their repertoire of organizers and choose one best suited to the activity at hand.

As visual representations of information, graphic organizers are powerful tools. They paint images on the brain (blueprints or maps). These images facilitate long-term memory and thereby increase comprehension and recall. Graphic organizers are brain-compatible tools that help students connect what they already know to what they are learning.

Graphic organizers . . .

- provide a way to organize information;

- help locate, select, sequence, and integrate information; and

- restructure information so that learned concepts can be applied and transferred to new situations.

As you look at the strategies and activities in this chapter, I want you to select the ones that use graphic organizers best suited to your content area and grade level. (Reproducible graphic organizers are in the back of the book and on the CD-ROM.) Consider the following questions:

1. Why am I asking students to use a graphic organizer?

    a. Will it be used as a study guide to help students study and prepare for assessment?

    b. Will it be used to show relationships to help students see connections between facts, concepts, events, or semantic information like words and places?

    c. Will it be used for assessment to evaluate what students have learned?

2. For the body of knowledge that I am teaching, what graphic organizer best matches the information that I want students to remember? (Choose the organizer based on the purpose. Don't just use a Venn diagram because you are familiar with it!)

3. How does the type of text (narrative or expository) affect students' use of the graphic organizer?

4. Will you have to modify the graphic organizer to fit the lesson, content, or grade level?

5. How can you relate the graphic organizer to real-life so students can see the value of using it in a variety of situations?

6. How can you use the graphic organizer to differentiate instruction?

How Can I Best Use the Strategies in this Chapter?

The following list is a quick reference to translate the research and the suggestions in previous chapters into practical pedagogy. Feel free to add to the list as you experience the power of the Nifty Fifty!

- Choose the ideas that fit well with the age and skill level of your students and are appropriate for their interests.

- Adapt any strategy to your own subject area and the needs of your students.

- Turn any strategy into a group discussion or small-group activity. As often as possible, provide time for students to share and defend their work and choices.

- Take time to model the strategy by using an example and working through it with the entire group. Project the graphic organizer, the words, or any other visual tools.

- Mix up strategies so students will stay motivated by surprise and freshness of a different type of activity.

- Return to a strategy that works well, using it with different content.

- If students are having a hard time with a concept or group of words, don't hesitate to try more than one strategy. Differentiate instruction by fitting strategies to individuals when needed.

- Many of the strategies and activities involve drawing. Remember that creating graphic images is not easy for all students. Always give students the option to create a symbol, diagram, stick-figure representation, or word description as an alternative to drawing a cartoon or picture.

- To keep the learning active, mix in one of the games now and then. Add movement to any of the strategies by grouping students in pairs—requiring them to move around the room—or taking time for students to roam and share or switch locations and share-discuss their ideas.

The Nifty Fifty!

So here are 50 of my favorite strategies for helping students learn academic vocabulary. These strategies work in any content area and at any grade level. Feel free to modify or extend the strategies—add your own style. Most are adaptations of tried and true best practices. The strategies provide ideas for presenting and then reinforcing academic vocabulary. In their book, *Bringing Words to Life: Robust Vocabulary Instruction*, Beck, McKeown, and Kucan describe several activities from their research as simple ways to introduce students to new vocabulary and then have them deal with the meanings right away. As all teachers do when they like and use someone else's ideas, I have taken their ideas and expanded upon some of them. You will find some of these ideas and those of many others mixed in throughout the strategies, activities, and games in this chapter. Where possible, I have given credit to the person(s) who seem to be the author of the idea. But many of these strategies have been used so often and with so many variations that it is impossible to know where the idea originated! (Like teachers before you, "borrow them straight" or "borrow and adjust" to fit your own needs.)

> *"The challenge for the content-area teacher is to determine what strategies will help students acquire the content knowledge while managing the wide range of differences in reading achievement."*
>
> David Sousa, 2005

Strategy 1

Vocabulary Notebooks

My favorite foldable is one that helps students create vocabulary notebooks using their own notebook paper. *Note: Scissors are needed for this activity.*

This vocabulary page provides students with a novel and engaging way to keep their vocabulary terms in their own notebooks. Many students who hate keeping vocabulary notebooks (pages where they have written words, definitions, and sentences) like doing this kind of page because it is different. The words students add to the page can be terms pretaught by the teacher or others students self-select from their reading. As they learn more about the words, I have students go back and add to their tabs synonyms, antonyms, or whatever I think will extend their understanding.

Step by Step

1. Do not remove the page from your notebook. Fold the right edge of one page over to the red line on the left side by the holes.

2. Starting on the left edge of the flap you created, use a scissors to cut about every third or fourth line over to the fold. This will make a series of tabs.

3. On the top of each tab, write a new word or concept.

4. Open the tab and write the meaning of the term or concept in your own words on the left. On the right of the fold, draw a picture or some kind of graphic representation to remind you what the word means. (This is something that would help you with the word meaning if you did not have the definition to help you.)

Vocabulary Placemat

This foldable or graphic organizer is an easy way to help students make connections between their prior knowledge and the new vocabulary. Since it is fun and easy to do, students like the process. (Follow the instructions below for making your own or use the graphic organizer labeled Strategy 2.) Whether you use that organizer or have students make their own, print or create the categories on both sides so that students can keep two terms or concepts at the same time, or laminate the place mats for multiple uses.

Step by Step

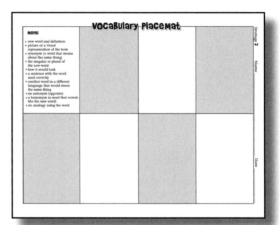

1. Give students copies of the graphic organizer for Strategy 2. (Or have them make their own placements by folding a sheet of paper into eight blocks.)

2. Label the first block: *The Word and Definition* (or *The Concept and Meaning*).

3. Label the remaining blocks. Choose from a menu of such possibilities as:

   a. new word

   b. picture or a visual representation of the term

   c. synonym (a word that means about the same thing)

   d. the singular or plural of the new word

   e. how it would look

   f. a sentence with the word used correctly

   g. another word in a different language that would mean the same thing (ESL students)

   h. an antonym

   i. an analogy using the word

   j. a homonym (a word that sounds like the new word)

Class Note Flipbook

Flipbooks are an easy way to keep information as notes or as part of a review. This foldable strategy is excellent for vocabulary and key terms and can be used in a variety of ways. Always remember that you can make flipbooks with any number of tabs that you need. For instance, you could have tabs for the layers of the earth, parts of speech, the planets, the branches of government, steps in a recipe, or for the parts of a car engine. One of my favorites is a flipbook with eight tabs for critical concepts or terms and the notes about those concepts or terms.

Flipbooks provide a novel and engaging way to take notes, and I've found that students are more likely to take notes using this format. I must confess that the reason I use eight tabs is that I can explain and model it easily for my students and I don't have to be mathematical and figure out what to do to get odd numbers on the tabs. *(I'm not a tactile learner and learning this foldable stuff was hard for me!)*

Step by Step

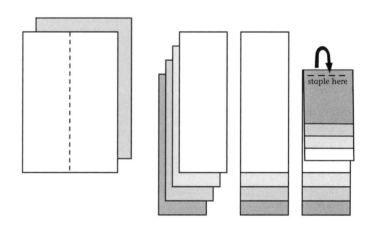

1. Fold two sheets of paper hot-dog style and tear them in half to make four sheets of long paper.

2. Put the four sheets together so the bottoms and tops are even. Slide each of the top three sheets up until the bottom of each of the four sheets has about one-half inch showing. (If you have done this correctly, when you hold the sheets and turn them over, you'll see the same half-inch difference showing at the top of the sheets on the other side.)

3. Fold the tops of the sheets down so that the half-inch tabs show all the way down the book. There will now be eight tabs that can be labeled and flipped up to use for vocabulary study.

4. Staple the top to make the pages stay together.

5. Label the tabs with important vocabulary words or concepts. Lift up the tabs. Add notes and visuals about the word in the blank space.

> *If you're not familiar with foldables and want more information, Dinah Zike has many resources that you can refer to for help. Don't forget to check your textbook's teacher edition, too. A number of textbook publishers are suggesting these special flipbooks in their teachers' guides.*

Strategy 4

Big Idea Circle

(Adapted from Concept Circles, Vacca, Vacca, and Grove Concept Circles 1987)

Concept circles help students categorize words or concepts and make connections among them. The circle graphic organizer provides a visual that helps students discuss, think, or write about content. This tool lets the teacher see the connections students are able to make from their learning about a given concept.

Step by Step

1. Start with the graphic organizer for Strategy 4.

2. Write a word or phrase in each section.

3. Make copies of this organizer (after your additions) for your students. (As an alternative, students can draw a large circle, divide it into four equal sections, and write the word in the sections.)

4. Students define each of the words or phrases. Then, they describe or name the concept to which all the sections relate. To do this, students have to examine the meanings of all the words, analyze the connection among the words, and think of a concept or relationship that ties the words together. Tell them to write the label or description in the center circle.

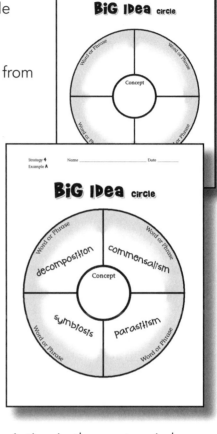

Or reverse the process:

1. YOU fill in the center of the circle with a concept before copying and distributing the graphic organizer.

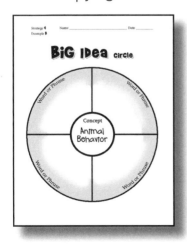

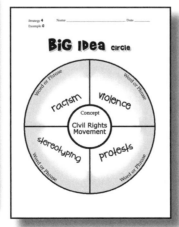

2. Ask students to complete the concept circle with four key vocabulary terms necessary to understanding the concept or four things they learned in relation to this concept. As an option, students can add definitions of the words.

How to Teach Academic Vocabulary

Connect Two

(Blachowicz & Lee, 1991)

This simple strategy can be used in a variety of ways. It deepens students' understandings of new terms or concepts and encourages them to think creatively about what the terms mean. The graphic organizer can be used to preteach vocabulary, provide review, or as a formative assessment. Students simply connect two words that have something in common and explain how and why they made their connections. Encourage students to think of connections that make sense to them.

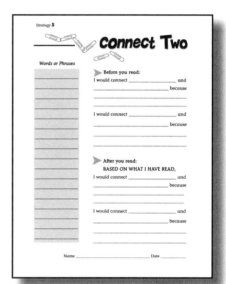

Step by Step

1. Select 10 to 15 words or phrases that are important for students to know prior to a reading selection.

2. Write the list on a copy of the graphic organizer for Strategy 5 or list the words on chart paper, chalkboard, overhead transparency, or computer projection for students to copy on cards or small pieces of paper.

3. Read the list of words with students.

4. Put students in pairs and ask them to "connect two" (choose two words they think might belong together) and state the reason for making the connection: "I would connect _____ and _____ because _____."

5. At this point in the process, it is important to stress to students that there are no right answers.
   Note: Modeling or demonstrating the procedure is also easier if the words are on small strips of an overhead transparency. The entire class can see the strips as you manipulate the pairs of words. It is okay if some words have several pairings or if students cannot find a connection for some words. Allow time for students to pair the words. Circulate around the room asking for the connections they are making.

6. Students read the selection.

7. Review the word list. Then ask students to make connections based on what they have read. Some of the connections will stay the same, and some will change.

   Have them share any new connections:

   "Based on what I read, I would connect _____ and _____ because _____."

8. To extend the activity, have students share with other pairs what they changed, if anything, and why.

On the Other Hand

On the Other Hand is a variation of *Connect Two* (previous page). Once again, students make connections among targeted terms or concepts, but this time the teacher structures the purpose. I like to have students cut and paste the words to get them engaged and motivated. This also provides a mind-body connection to move the ideas into long-term memory. It takes a little longer but it is well worth the time spent, especially on difficult terms or concepts.

Step by Step

1. Give students a list of paired words with opposite meanings (or concepts with contrasting implications) and a copy of the graphic organizer for Strategy 6.

2. Students write the opposite words in the appropriate spot on the left- and right-hand graphic.

3. Give each pair of students a stack of newspapers and magazines. Students choose a pair of words and work together to find and cut out pictures, cartoons, words, or phrases that could represent the words or concepts.

4. They glue the pictures, words, or phrases onto the corresponding hand-shaped space on the graphic.

5. Students then go "pair to square" (two pairs join together). In the group of four, each pair explains their pictures and what they were thinking as they used them to represent the terms. This step serves as a valuable tool for assessing whether students actually have a working knowledge of particular words.

Yes? or No?

(adapted from the Frayer Model, Frayer, Frederick & Klausmeier, 1969)

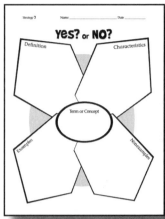

The **Yes? or No?** model (an adaptation of the Frayer Model) is a word categorization activity that helps students learn attributes and nonattributes and give examples and nonexamples of challenging words. The model provides a graphic framework for students to do this. Students return to the model a number of times, adding and removing the entries as they deepen their understanding of the vocabulary during the lesson or unit. In order to refine their understanding of a term, students must know what it is not, as well as what it is.

Make sure you model this graphic organizer with students so they can apply the thinking strategy for themselves when they encounter new or difficult terms and ideas. This graphic organizer works well with all age groups.

Step by Step

1. Give students copies of the graphic organizer for Strategy 7. Define the new word for them in student-friendly terms.

2. Distinguish between the new term and similar terms students already know that might be confused with the new term.

3. Give examples of the new term and explain why they are examples.

4. Give nonexamples and explain why they are not examples of the new term.

5. Give students more examples and nonexamples and ask them to distinguish between them. Make sure that students explain their thinking (*metacognition*). Students can write all the examples and nonexamples in the appropriate spot on the graphic organizer.

6. Have students add their own examples and nonexamples and explain to a partner why they are one or the other.

7. As a class, talk about some of the examples and nonexamples and provide feedback about the choices.

Variation of the Yes? or No? Model

This model can be used as readily to define and understand bigger concepts. Follow the same steps as for vocabulary terms. This time broaden the discussion to essential and nonessential characteristics, as well as examples and nonexamples.

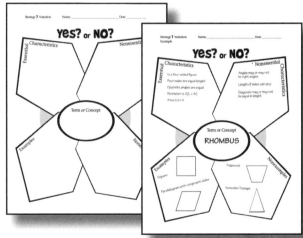

How to Teach Academic Vocabulary
©Copyright Incentive Publications, Inc., Nashville, TN

Strategy 8

How Well Do I Know These Words?

This graphic organizer strategy encourages students to work with each other to develop clear understandings of important terms. Students must analyze whether they know a word and then whether they know the term well enough to teach it to someone else.

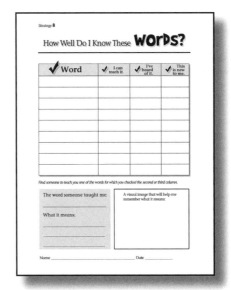

Step by Step

1. Make a copy of the graphic organizer for Strategy 8. In the left-hand column, write the list of vocabulary terms you want students to consider.

2. Make copies of this organizer (after your additions) for your students.

3. Students work through the list of words, considering and identifying their level of understanding of each word according to the categories in the three right-hand columns.

   - A term I understand so well that I can teach it to someone else
   - A term I've heard, but I'm not sure what it means
   - A term that is new to me and someone will need to teach it to me

4. As students complete the chart, direct them to find someone who can teach one of the terms for which they had a check in the third or fourth column.

5. Students then write the new understanding of the term and draw an image to help them remember what the term means.

Illustrate and Associate

This strategy uses visualization and personalization to help students learn vocabulary words or key concepts. The graphic organizer leads students to create a concrete connection to the vocabulary words or key concepts. It also leads them to a personal connection. This often provides more meaning to students than a technical or confusing dictionary definition.

Step by Step

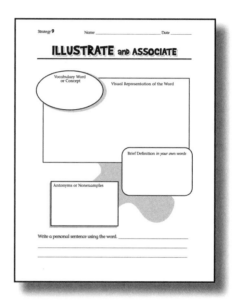

1. Give students copies of the graphic organizer for Strategy 9.

2. Students write the vocabulary term in the oval.

3. They fill in the shapes on the graphic organizer, associating the word with a visual image and an antonym or nonexample of the word.

4. Finally, students write a sentence that associates the word with a personal experience or meaning.

List-Group-Label

(adapted from Taba, 1967)

List-Group-Label is a three-step vocabulary strategy that is helpful to use near the end of a unit or lesson. This graphic organizer requires students to actively and visually reorganize what they have learned, and makes it easier for them to understand and remember the information. The strategy stresses the interrelationships among technical vocabulary words and engages students with the content. It requires linking prior knowledge to the new learning.

Step by Step

1. Give students copies of the graphic organizer for Strategy 10.

2. **List**—Students brainstorm all the words they have learned in association to a major topic they have been studying. (Do this as a group.) Record all the words until you have a list of 20 or more words.

3. **Group**—Students work together in pairs or triads to rearrange the words into categories or groups. There is no need to worry about the names of the categories at this point, since the goal is to group words that have connections to each other.

4. **Label**—Students then give a label to each category of words to identify the connections among the terms. Some of the words in the chosen categories may not fit when a label is given, so students can suggest another category label for the leftover terms.

5. When the categories have been labeled, students discuss how the labels fit and whether additional terms can be added to any of the groups.

Puzzle It

Content puzzles help students take notes and remember information. The graphic organizer provides a way for students to distinguish between key concepts and subordinate ideas in the text. The puzzle headings provide students with a focus for the reading.

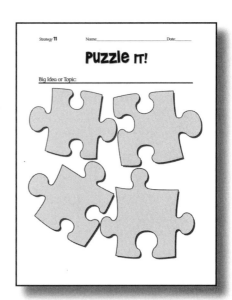

Step by Step

1. Give students copies of the Puzzle It! graphic organizer for Strategy 11.

2. Before students read in depth, ask them to skim the text and make a list of important ideas. These can be teacher-directed when you model the strategy.

3. Students write one subtopic on one of the pieces of the graphic organizer (important people, major battles, war strategies, important terms).

4. As students read, they write (onto the appropriate puzzle piece) the words or phrases from the text that fit each category.

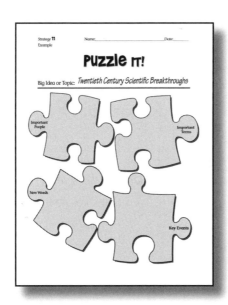

How to Teach Academic Vocabulary
©Copyright Incentive Publications, Inc., Nashville, TN

Strategy 12

P.A.V.E. the Way

P.A.V.E. the Way allows students to identify unknown vocabulary based on their prior knowledge about the terms or based on the context of the unknown word. You can use P.A.V.E. as an individual assignment or as a group activity. Be sure to demonstrate the technique to the entire group.

Step by Step

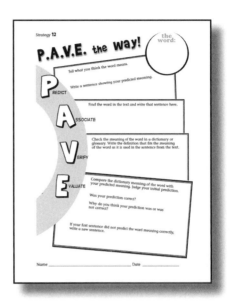

1. Make a copy of the graphic organizer for Strategy 12. Project this, choose a term students are learning, and work as a class to complete the P.A.V.E. process as a sample for students.

2. Give students copies of the graphic organizer. Give them an unknown vocabulary term to write in the circle on the upper right. (You can give different words to different students.)

3. Students then follow the P.A.V.E path on their own.

4. When graphic organizers are complete, allow time for students to share their words and understandings with a few other students until all the words have been reviewed.

Strategy 13

On Close Inspection

(Adapted from Johnson & Pearson, 1984; Baldwin, Ford & Readance, 1981; Baumann, Kameenuie, & Ash, 2003)

This strategy leads students to do feature analysis—useful when a cluster of new terms represents members of the same categories. Feature analysis helps students figure out a term's meaning by comparing its features to other terms that fall into the same category or class. The strategy requires students to consider features that the item or idea represented by a vocabulary term might or might not possess. They complete a semantic feature matrix, creating a visual summary of concept features and showing how certain terms are alike or different. (Remember that we have generations of kids who think that *compare and contrast* is one word because of the way that most of us teach the terms! This graphic organizer is an excellent way to help them gain deeper understanding of the concept of comparison.)

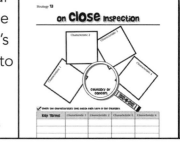

Step by Step

1. Select a general category of study. Choose concrete concepts (remember scaffolding) such as healthy foods, animal breeds, geometric shapes. After you begin teaching the strategy and students become adept at using this model, they can analyze more sophisticated or abstract categories such as forms of government, types of poultry feed, land forms, and polygons.

2. Make a copy of the graphic organizer for Strategy 13. Fill in the characteristics on the upper portion, above the matrix.

3. Make copies of this organizer (after your additions) for your students. They can use a checkmark to indicate if the feature applies to the vocabulary term. Some teachers use the letter *S* if a concept sometimes has that feature.

4. Students work in pairs and explain the thinking behind their choices. Explain this metacognition (putting into words their analysis and listening to others' thinking). Doing so enhances understanding of the concepts and helps put the information into long-term memory.

5. As understanding of terms deepens during the lesson, students add terms and features to the matrix.

6. As an extension, students could write definitions of the terms based on the information from the charts. The definitions should include the category and distinguishable features. This is an excellent way to help students use writing to better understand the terms. If they compare their definitions to a glossary or dictionary, they may find that they are similar!

Words on a Scale

A semantic scale is a very simple diagram—a straight line—used to show relationships among words that vary in degree. The scale is anchored at each end by a word familiar to the students. The words are antonyms. New words are written on the scale in an appropriate place after they are introduced and discussed. This graphic organizer offers a visual representation of the scale. The main advantage of semantic scales is that they allow new academic terms to be reinforced in related clusters to aid in retention and to deepen understanding of the word meanings. Having pairs of students work together to create semantic scales is an effective way for students to process their thinking. There may be disagreements among students about the best place to put a word on the scale, and the more they discuss the varying degrees of meaning of the term, the more it becomes part of long-term memory. Semantic scales are also useful when examining positive and negative meanings of words even though their definitions are nearly the same. This approach is simple and effective for deepening students' word knowledge after the words have been studied.

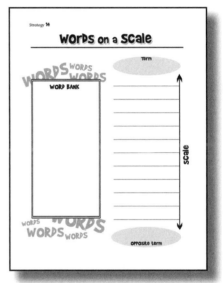

Step by Step

1. Make a copy of the graphic organizer for Strategy 14. Write the words in the word bank and write antonym labels at each end of the scale.

2. Make copies of this organizer (after your additions) for your students.

3. Students work in pairs to place the terms on the scale in appropriate places.

4. Take time for student pairs to share the completed scales with another pair or with the class, and for a discussion of the reasons for placement on the scales.

Examples of Semantic Scales:

A. Place these words on the scale from hot to cold:
   sweltering, frigid, tepid, chilly, warm, lukewarm, glacial, blistering, fiery, numbing, searing, cool, crisp, nippy, sizzling.

B. Place these words on the scale from positive to negative connotations of thin:
   skinny, trim, slender, emaciated, svelte, thin, emaciated, bony, beanstalk, delicate, lanky, lean, scrawny, starved, wan, wasted, puny.

The Clunk Bus

The **Clunk Bus** strategy requires students to identify the vocabulary words they have trouble understanding when they are reading text. (When the bus has a problem on the road, it clunks.) The graphic organizer helps students to identify an unknown word and to search the sentence in which the word is located for clues to the word's meaning. Students use the context clues to construct their own definition of the unknown word so they can continue reading. (The bus can begin clicking along the road again.) You can have students do this individually as they read and then put them into pairs to compare words. Or students can read a portion of text and then work together to complete the graphic organizer.

Step by Step

1. Give students copies of the graphic organizer for Strategy 15. Students can work in pairs or do this individually and pair up later to discuss their work.

2. Student writes each "clunk" word on a bus.

3. For each clunk word, the student looks in the sentence for clues about the word's meaning and writes these clues (key words) on the spaces in the bus—such as windows and tires. (Students do not need to fill in all spots.)

4. Based on the clues, students write a definition sentence that shows the meaning of the word.

5. Create a Clunk Bus Word Wall by placing a large paper bus on the wall. Students can add their "clunk" words to the bus. Have fun mastering all the words on the Class Clunk Bus.

How to Teach Academic Vocabulary
©Copyright Incentive Publications, Inc., Nashville, TN

Strategy 16

TIP: Term, Information, Picture

TIP is another way for students to fully integrate the meaning of the key term or concept into their memories. By making a simple sketch that explains the key idea, students synthesize and interpret the new information and make it their own. Students can refer to their drawings to easily remember new key ideas. Remember that drawing is not easy for all students, so encourage them to use any kind of visual diagram or symbols, in addition to drawings, to help them remember the term.

Step by Step

1. Give students copies of the TIP graphic organizer for Strategy 16.

2. Students write the key idea or term (T) and the information or definition (I) that goes with it. Finally, they draw a visual memory clue (P).

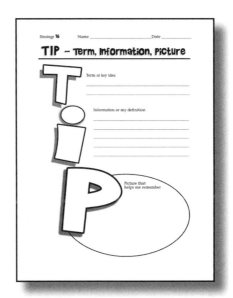

   T: The *term* is the new vocabulary word or a new concept.

   I: The *information* is a definition or it may be a more technical explanation of the concept.

   P: The *picture* or memory clue is a way for students to fully integrate the meaning of the key term or concept into their memories.

It's in the Cards

Vocabulary prediction is an instructional strategy that encourages students to think about key terms or concepts by having them do a series of structured steps. There are many variations of this prereading activity to help students get an initial understanding of new terms or concepts before they read the text. These prediction activities (Strategies 17, 18, and 19) get students actively engaged in learning the word and help them analyze correct usage and effective word choice.

The idea is to hook the kids on wanting to know what the words or concepts mean so they will want to read the text to see if what they have predicted is correct. Most kids think they know something about just about everything *(they've heard it on TV, from their friends or parents, or on the Internet—and we know how reliable these sources are)*, so these activities give students a way to show what they think they know and then have an opportunity to argue about what they think. What more could a teacher want from an activity—kids who want to read and argue!

Step by Step

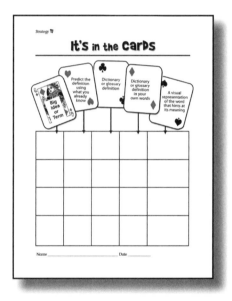

1. Before students read, select from the text about ten words (five to seven for younger students) that are colorful, unusual, or unfamiliar. Provide these words in a visual format near the front of the room where students can easily see them or give students a copy of the list. Group the words by parts of speech, relationships, synonyms and antonyms, or randomly.

2. Give students copies of the graphic organizer for Strategy 17. As a class, review the meanings of familiar words. Then, they can work as a class, alone, or in pairs (depending on their developmental level) to make guesses (predictions) about the new words.

4. After they make their predictions and write them down, students look the words up in the dictionary or glossary and rewrite the definition in their own words. Finally, they create some sort of a visual representation of the word. This can be as simple as spelling out the word—writing it in a way and shape that hints at the meaning.

5. After reading, students go back to the list and identify how the author actually used the words. Discuss such questions as: "Did the author use the words effectively?" and "Would you have used words differently to make the word meanings more clear?"

How to Teach Academic Vocabulary
©Copyright Incentive Publications, Inc., Nashville, TN

It's Predictable!

The ***It's Predictable*** strategy is a variation of the prediction exercise in Strategy 17. Students make predictions before reading the text, then revise their predictions after reading. In addition, they think about what clues in the text helped to clarify their understanding of the words. The organizer has room for them to work on two different words.

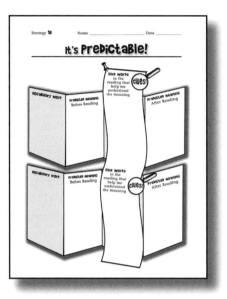

Step by Step

1. Give students copies of the graphic organizer for Strategy 18.

2. Provide a list of words from the text that you want students to learn.

3. Students write unfamiliar words, along with their predicted meanings.

4. Next, students read the selection. As they read, they identify and note clues in the text that help them understand the word meanings.

5. Finally, students revise their predictions about the meanings of the words.

6. Allow time for students to discuss why they changed their predictions.

Fiction Predictions

The **Fiction Predictions** strategy uses a graphic organizer to lead students in using words from a fiction selection to make predictions about the selection. Students assign the words to different categories of story elements, then use the word groupings to help them think about story possibilities.

Step by Step

1. Make a copy of the graphic organizer for Strategy 19.

2. Create a list of key words from the story and write them in the word bank at the top of the graphic organizer. (Be sure to choose words that would fall into the categories of setting, characters, plot, conflict, or resolution.)

3. Give copies of the organizer to students.

4. Before reading the passage, students place each word in the story element category in which they predict the author will use the words.

5. Then encourage further predictions by asking these guiding questions. These will ensure that your students understand the literary elements on the graphic organizer and will lead them to make predictions about the story. Students can write notes on the back of the page or just discuss these questions orally.

   Setting—Based on the words you selected for setting, what can you predict about the setting for the story?

   Characters—Based on the words you selected for the setting, what can you predict about the characters from these words?

   Plot—Based on the words you selected, what do you think will happen in the story?

   Conflict—Based on words you selected for the conflict, what do you predict the main story problem or conflict will be?

   Resolution—Based on the words you selected, what do your predict about the story ending?

   Questions—Based on the entire group of words given, what questions do you have about the story?

6. Completely unfamiliar words can be listed in the Mystery Words section of the graphic organizer.

7. After reading, students revisit their graphic organizer to answer the questions they wrote, define mystery words, and revise their predictions.

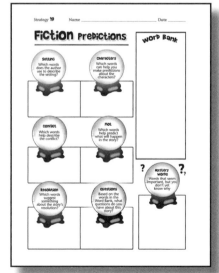

How to Teach Academic Vocabulary
©Copyright Incentive Publications, Inc., Nashville, TN

Nonfiction Predictions

This variation of this strategy uses a similar graphic organizer to lead students in using words from a nonfiction selection to make predictions about the text. Students assign the words to different categories or elements of the passage, then use the word groupings to help them think about what they will learn from the passage.

Step by Step

1. Make a copy of the graphic organizer for Strategy 19, Variation (nonfiction).

2. Create a list of key words from the story and write them in the word bank at the top of the graphic organizer. (Be sure to choose words that would fall into the categories of setting, characters, plot, conflict, or resolution.)

3. Give copies of the organizer to students.

4. Before reading the passage, students place each word in the category in which they predict the author will use the words.

5. Encourage further predictions by asking these guiding questions. These will push students to deeper thought and discussion of their choices and build anticipation for reading the passage. They will want to see if they are right about their predictions and find out how those words area actually used in the passage. Students can write notes on the back of the page or just discuss these questions orally.

   Purpose—Based on the words you selected for purpose, what can you predict about the purpose of the passage?

   Audience—Based on the words you selected for the audience, who do you think the author intended the audience to be?

   Main thesis or idea—Based on the words you selected for the main idea, what do you think will be the thesis or major point of the passage?

   Supporting facts or argument—Based on words you selected for the supporting facts, what ideas, facts, or arguments do you think the author will use to make the main point?

   Conclusion—Based on the words you selected for conclusion, how do you think the author will end the passage?

   Questions—Based on the entire group of words given in the word bank, what questions do you have about the passage?

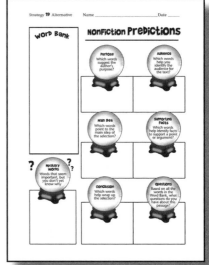

6. Completely unfamiliar words can be listed in the Mystery Words section of the graphic organizer.

7. After reading, students revisit their graphic organizer to answer the questions they wrote, define mystery words, and revise their predictions.

Strategy 20

Word Spiral

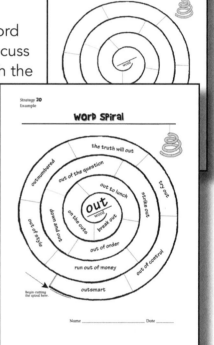

The **Word Spiral** graphic organizer gives students a way to collect and discuss word usages that they recognize, as well as learn usages they do not know or fully understand. Students' finished products will contain a collection of uses of one word, beginning with the uses they frequently employ, and spiraling down to newer or more complex usages. There are many words that have multiple meanings. Some of these are simple words that seem easy to know and understand—words such as *out, time, down, run, up,* and many others. As simple as they seem, however, their uses in expressions, phrases, idioms, or other figures of speech are often confusing. To understand meanings of written passages, students need to have full understanding of the many uses of words in their language.

Step by Step

1. Make a copy of the graphic organizer for Strategy 20.

2. Demonstrate the strategy to the class. Begin with a word that is common to many expressions (such as **run**). Discuss some definitions of the word **run** itself. Brainstorm with the class to gather expressions that use the word. (They might suggest such things as *home run, run-around, run like the wind, run for office, in the long run, run for your life, well-run, run the water, feeling run-down,* and so on.) Write these on the spiral. Near the end of the spiral, you add expressions such as *a run of bad luck, a newspaper run, run off some fliers, runoff election, erosion runoff, run of the mill, give me a rundown,* and more.) As you work, discuss the meanings of all the expressions.

3. Give students copies of the graphic organizer.

4. Give them a word with multiple uses or a selection of words from which they can choose.

5. Students work in pairs to collect and write expressions.

6. Follow the directions on the graphic organizer to carefully cut the spirals.
   Note: Once the spirals are cut, students can write more phrases on the backs of the spiral.

7. Share the collected phrases and clarify the meanings. Have students give a situation in which each expression might be used.

8. Punch a hole in the top and hang these from the ceiling, a clothesline, the edges of desks or somewhere else in the room.

9. Encourage students to watch for these expressions in their reading.

Words Take Flight

Words Take Flight is a strategy that gets students up, out of their seats, and moving. This actively engages students as they create the foldable helicopters, choose words to review, drop the helicopters from the sky, scramble to catch someone else's helicopter, and write definitions, synonyms, or antonyms for the word on another helicopter. All these actions help to store the word meanings in long-term memory!

Step by Step

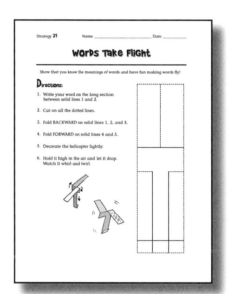

1. Prepare a list of words with which you want students to engage more deeply. You can put these on small pieces of paper in a basket.

2. Each student chooses one of the words.

3. Give students copies of the helicopter pattern on graphic Strategy 21.

4. BEFORE students make the helicopters, instruct them to write their word in the long space between solid lines 1 and 2.

5. Then students follow directions to make the helicopter. Then can lightly color or decorate the helicopters.

6. Students stand up on their chairs and drop the helicopters. They must catch someone else's helicopter and write a definition for the word on the flat, wider section (the section that is just below the "wings").

7. They drop the helicopter again. This time, they must catch yet another helicopter and write a synonym on one of the wings (rotors). Label that word **syn** for synonym.

8. They drop the helicopter again. This time, they must catch a different helicopter and write an antonym for the main word on the other wing (rotor). Label that word **ant** for antonym.

9. After this, you can make an attempt to get each helicopter back into the hands of the first person who made it.

Wonder Wheel

The **Wonder Wheel** strategy pushes students to think and connect more deeply with the meaning of a word. It asks questions that require students to think about the wider uses, influences, consequences, and implications of a word or to consider the idea, action, thing, experience, or attribute named by the word.

Step by Step

1. Make a copy of the graphic organizer for Strategy 22. Write a sample word in the center of the wheel and project the copy.

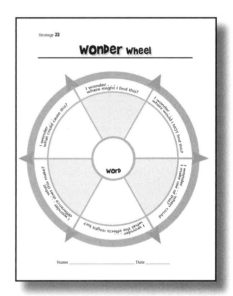

2. Work with the class to brainstorm ideas for completing the wheel. This models critical thinking and expansion of the word meaning. On the question, "What difference does this make?" ask students to think about how the idea, event, or thing represented by the word affects the world, their lives, or other people. An alternative question might be, "What influences does this have?"

3. Give students copies of the graphic organizer, along with words for them to expand. You might give different words to each student or student pair.

4. Students work to complete the word wheels.

5. Allow time for them to share and explain their ideas.

Digging Deeper

Digging Deeper, like the *Wonder Wheel* of Strategy 22, pushes students to think and connect more deeply with the meaning of a word. This strategy requires students to think about the wider uses, influences, consequences, and implications of a word or to consider the idea, action, thing, experience, or attribute named by the word. In addition, it engages students personally with the word by asking them to think about how it relates to their lives.

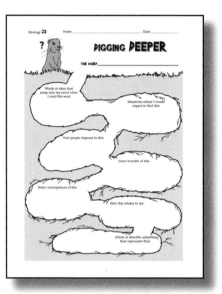

Step by Step

1. Make a copy of the graphic organizer for Strategy 23. Write a sample word and definition and project the copy.

2. Work with the class to brainstorm ideas for completing the layers. This models critical thinking and expansion of the word meaning.

3. Give students copies of the graphic organizer, along with words for them to expand. You might give different words to each student or student pair.

4. Students work to complete the layers.

5. Allow time for them to share and explain their ideas.

Vocabulary Pyramid

Vocabulary Pyramids can be made up of as many blocks as the teacher would like to use. Each block is a different activity using the targeted terms. This strategy can be used as a vocabulary station (center), or pyramids can be culminating projects (in place of the traditional matching, multiple choice, or fill-in-the-blank vocabulary test).

Step by Step

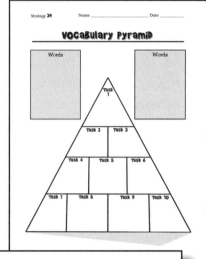

1. Choose the vocabulary pyramid outline you want to use (see the graphic organizers labeled Strategy 24 or Strategy 24, Variation). Make a copy of this for yourself.

2. Fill in the list of 10 to 15 words that you want students to learn or review.

3. Fill in your selected tasks.

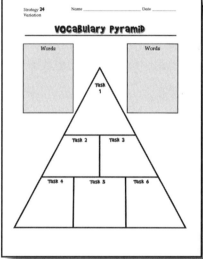

4. Give copies of the graphic organizer (pyramid) to students.

5. All students must complete the top of the pyramid (Task 1).

6. Each student selects a specified number of the remaining blocks of the pyramid. (You choose this number.) At least one of the blocks must be done alone, and one must be done with a partner or two other people. Students can color in the blocks as they complete the tasks.

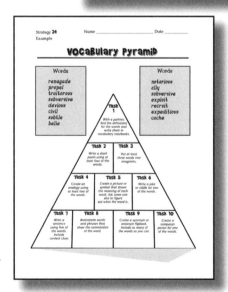

7. Students can do their work on separate sheets of paper and staple the pyramid to the front of their work.

How to Teach Academic Vocabulary
©Copyright Incentive Publications, Inc., Nashville, TN

Note: Remember to use or create a pyramid to hold an appropriate number of activities for your students. Since students have choice, include tasks at different levels of complexity and tasks that take different kinds of thinking or processing. Be sure to make some individual activities, as well as some for students to work in pairs or triads. Here are a few ideas for pyramid tasks. You can add many variations to the list:

Definitions—With a partner, find the definitions for the words and write them in your vocabulary notebooks.

Synonyms—Choose four words. For each one, find two words that have a similar meaning to that vocabulary word.

Antonyms—Choose four words. For each one, find three words that mean the opposite of that vocabulary word.

Flipbook—Create a synonym or antonym flipbook. Include as many of the words as you can.

Flashcards—Create flashcards for seven of the words with a picture on one side and a definition on the other.

Picture or Symbol—Create a picture or symbol that shows the meaning of each word. Share your pictures with a partner and see if he or she can figure out what word each one represents.

Sentences—Write a sentence using five of the words. Include context clues.

Sentence Story—Write a short story using all of the vocabulary words. Underline each word as you use it.

Crossword Puzzle—Create a puzzle for 7 words. Use the definitions as clues for *Down* and *Across*.

Puns, Jokes, or Riddles—Write a pun, joke, or riddle for at least two of the words.

Analogies—Create an analogy using at least two of the words.

Anagrams—Put at least three words into anagrams.

Connotations—Brainstorm words and phrases that show the connotation of the word.

Unlocking Analogies

This strategy taps into students' association and comprehension-processing levels. It is intended to help students identify synonyms, antonyms, and analogies for key vocabulary that has been identified for instruction. Word associations, particularly analogies, can be challenging for students.

(Hey, analogies are challenging for teachers! If you use this strategy, it will help you become better with analogies yourself. You've got to love it when teaching kids helps us become smarter, too.)

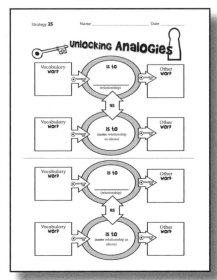

Word association using analogies is very important for comprehension and should be started in early grades.

When you begin analogies for students at any grade level, you must introduce them using simple concepts. Select analogies that initially use synonyms and antonyms and either whole-to-part or part-to-whole associations (scaffolding). When you give analogies, you must model analogy completion by thinking aloud (metacognition) so that students learn the rationale for the word chosen to complete the analogy. The graphic organizer will give students a visual pattern to help them see the relationships in an analogy.

Step by Step

1. Teach students how to work with analogies. Begin by explaining that analogies examine and repeat word relationships. Each one contains two terms in the first set that have the same relationship as the two terms in the second set: A is to B as C is to D; instruction is to learning as construction is to building.

2. Create analogies where one term is missing and let students finish the statement that will complete the analogy.

3. Students identify and explain the relationship between the first two items and then apply that relationship to the second set of items.

4. Once students can do analogies with one term missing, move to analogies where two terms are missing.

5. Students will need multiple experiences with teacher-created analogies before they can develop their own. (This is one time where scaffolding is essential even for our best and brightest students.)

6. There are a wide variety of analogy categories (kinds of relationships) that you'll want to teach students as they learn how to develop association and comprehension processing. Use the ones that fit best with your content.

Synonyms . . . . .end : terminate

Antonyms . . . . .artificial : real

Worker and tool used . . . . .photographer : camera

Tool and object its used on . . . . .scissors : paper

Cause and effect . . . . .negligence : accident

Effect and cause . . . . tsunami : earthquake

Part to whole . . . . .leaf : tree

Function. . . . . .flagella : movement

Whole to Part. computer : keyboard

Age . . . . infant : adolescent

Symbol and what it stands for . . . . rose : love

Mathematical relationship . . . . .six : thirty-six

Attribute . . . . .diamond : hard

Classification and type . . . . dog : poodle

Degree of intensity . . . . cold : pneumonia

Worker and object created . . . . .artist : painting

Material used and end product . . . . lumber : house

Word form . . . . friend : friendship

7. Give students copies of the graphic organizer for Strategy 25. They can use the organizer to visually map out some analogies.

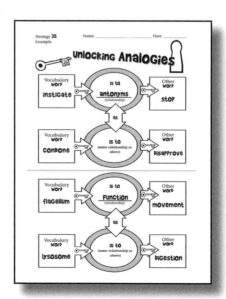

Word Map

(Schwartz & Raphael, 1985)

Word Maps (concept definition maps) are used to teach students the meanings of key concepts. They help students understand the essential attributes, qualities, or characteristics of a word's meaning and contrast these with irrelevant or nonessential characteristics. Students must describe what the concept is, is not, and cite examples. This process gives students a more thorough understanding of what the concept means, includes, and implies. The mapping process uses the power of visualization, so it aids with long-term memory.

Step by Step

1. Display an example of a concept or definition map. (Make a copy of the graphic organizer for Strategy 26 and project it or use the CD-ROM and project it.)

2. Discuss that a definition should answer these questions:

   a. What is it? (What broader category or classification of things does it fit into?)

   b. What is it like? (What are the essential characteristics? What qualities does it possess that make it different from other things in the same category?)

   c. What are some examples of it?

3. Model how to use the map by selecting a familiar vocabulary term from a previous unit and mapping its features.

   • Guide students to generate examples to illustrate the word or concept.

   • Guide students to identify relevant (essential) characteristics and contrast these with irrelevant (nonessential) characteristics.

   • Attach the concept to a larger category.

4. Select another familiar vocabulary term and volunteer information for a map.

5. Give students copies of the graphic organizers and a word or concept to map. Have them work in pairs to complete a map for a concept in the unit. They may use a dictionary or glossary but they can use what they already know as well.

6. After the maps are finished, have students write a complete definition of the concept in their own words using the information from their maps.

7. As the unit progresses, students can refine their maps as they learn additional characteristics and examples of the concept.

Word Cache

Too often, students are overwhelmed with the number of unknown words they encounter in their texts. They believe that every word is important, and if they don't know all of them, they shut down and decide that the reading is not worth doing and is too hard. This activity is useful to show students that we cannot know or teach every unfamiliar word that they see in their texts. The **Word Cache** graphic organizer gives students a visual nudge to become more word-conscious and selective in knowing which words are critical to understanding what they read in different content areas.

Step by Step

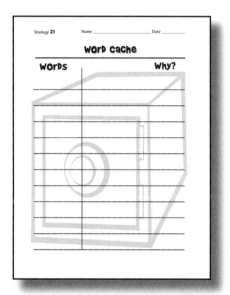

1. Give students copies of the graphic organizer for Strategy 27.

2. Students preview the text, then work in pairs or triads to develop a list of unfamiliar words that they believe will be crucial for understanding the focus of the unit. In the word cache, students write words, followed by a phrase (under Why?) that gives a clue as to why they believe the word is important for understanding the content.

3. Student-selected words can be transferred to a master class list, with each group of students defending its selections.

4. The teacher then helps students modify this list by deleting terms judged to be less important and adding any vocabulary concepts that students overlooked based on the knowledge of a content specialist. (Yes, the teacher is the expert.) The teacher clearly explains the reasons for including certain words and eliminating others so that students understand how to identify crucial words in content reading.

5. After vocabulary words are selected and students understand why these particular words and concepts are the most important to know, the teacher uses an appropriate vocabulary strategy to help them understand the word meanings and the relationship among the words.

Word Storm

Word Storm guides students in a variation of *Word Cache* (Strategy 27). Students gather words related to a major concept or a reading passage. Then the teacher uses guiding questions that help expand their word collection. Finally, students examine the lists and group words with commonalities.

Step by Step

1. Give students copies of the graphic organizer for Strategy 28.

2. In pairs, students list all the words they can think of that are related to the major topic or concept to be studied (major concept of text—composition and classification of fertilizers, basic food groups, land formations, and so forth). They list these words in the "storm" shape on the graphic organizer. (Colored markers work well.) As a variation have students write the words on paper, cut them out, and paste them onto the tornado to create a collage look.

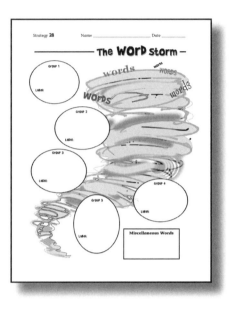

3. When students have exhausted their contributions, help them add to their lists by asking some guiding questions:

   • Can you think of a word that describes . . . ?

   • Can you think of words that would show how someone might see, hear, feel, touch, or smell when they are working with . . . or in a situation that involves . . . ?

   • What are some words made from this root (include this prefix or suffix) that we need to know?

4. Students then group the words they have listed by looking for words that have something in common.

5. Once words are grouped, direct students to decide on a label for each group. If they need more groups, they may draw more shapes on the front or back of the page. Tell them that they may have one category of Miscellaneous Words for no more than three or four words that don't fit in another group.

6. When students have completed the task and shared "pair to square," introduce any additional words that you feel should be included and have students add them to the right groups.

Word Splash

"Splash" a group of key words on a projection surface, a board, or the graphic organizer for Strategy 29. Students examine the group of words and use them to predict major ideas from a passage they will read. This strategy involves students in setting the purposes for reading, because their predictions will lead them to ideas about what to look for as they read. In addition, the strategy provides familiarity with the key vocabulary needed to understand the reading.

Step by Step

1. Write five to seven key words or terms on separate pieces of acetate and place them on an overhead projector or randomly write them on a surface to be projected on a white board or other projection device. The words should appear to be "splashed" on the surface. As an alternative, "splash" the words on a copy of the graphic organizer for Strategy 29.

2. Give students some information about the passage they are about to read (a story about _____, an instructive passage about _____).

3. In pairs, students write a sentence or two in which they try to use all the words to predict how the terms might be related to each other in the selection they are about to read. If they have no familiarity with some of the words, they may use a dictionary to find meanings.

4. Students then read the text to check the accuracy of their predictions.

5. If their predictions are not correct, students can revise their sentences.

Word Webs

Knowing some common prefixes, suffixes, and root words can help students learn the meaning of many new words. Prefixes are relatively easy to learn because they have clear meanings and are usually spelled the same way. If students learn the four most common prefixes, they will have important clues about the meanings of about two-thirds of all English words that have prefixes. Suffixes are slightly more difficult, but they are helpful to aid students in word meanings. Word Webs are useful, when investigating word families and using their shared 'meaning' parts to learn new words and word relatedness.

Step by Step

1. Give students copies of the graphic organizer for Strategy 30.

2. Choose a word part from a family (a root, prefix, or suffix). Students write it in the center of the web graphic organizer.

3. Discuss the meaning of the word part. If space allows, they can write the meaning in the center of the web along with the word.

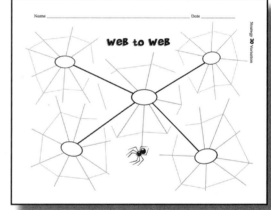

4. Write words that contain this same word part on the strands of the web.

5. Discuss the meaning of each word, including any prefixes, suffixes, or roots that may be contained in the word.

6. Students can then create a new word web for one of the prefixes, suffixes, or roots used in the first web. Connect the webs with the words that have both parts in common. (See the Web to Web graphic organizer, variation for Strategy 30.)

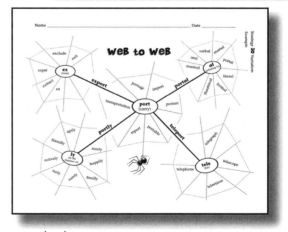

7. Discuss with students that words can belong to more than one family. Create new word webs for each prefix, suffix, and root family that is used in the first web. Connect the webs with the words that are in common.

How to Teach Academic Vocabulary
©Copyright Incentive Publications, Inc., Nashville, TN

Strategy 31

ABC Vocabulary Review

This vocabulary review is a simple foldable (or a graphic organizer) with an alphabetized list of words that pertain to a given unit of study. It is most useful when topics are broad based or where a large amount of information is included. It can be used before reading to check for background knowledge, during reading to note key terms or information, and after reading to create a summary or review of the knowledge gained. Before a unit test or culminating activity, students can use the sheet as a review of significant people, events, formulas, or terminology. Students can work alone, with a partner, or with a team developing the list.

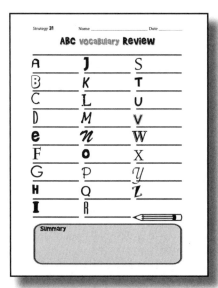

Step by Step

1. Students fold a piece of notebook paper in thirds lengthwise and list the letters of the alphabet down the left side of the columns, skipping a few lines each time so that they have plenty of room to write words or phrases. They can write A–I in the first column, J–R in the second column, and S–Z in the last column. Or you can give them copies of the graphic organizer for Strategy 31.

2. Beside each letter, students fill in words or phrases that are key to the content studied. They can fill in letters in any order. They do not have to go letter by letter. (Many times it will be difficult to use Q, X, and Z, so let students be creative! Your class is Xiting.)

3. Students can begin individually and then get into pairs or teams after everyone has had time to think.

4. Students share their lists with the class. If another pair or group has better words, then students may change theirs to the ones that are better. Remember, this is a review and the more information students get, the better they will understand the content.

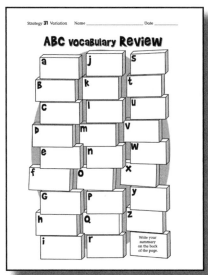

5. A final step could be to have students write a summary that includes the major terms, ideas, and concepts, or they could create a graphic organizer of what they have learned.

   Note: Announce to students that they will be able to use their ABC Review when they take the test. This is a great student motivator for quality work!

Applause! Applause!

This activity sounds so easy that teachers of older students might think it's too simple; but it is a very handy and quick formative assessment to see if students understand the new terms or know how to use them. Students are asked to clap (as many times as the teacher wants; I usually make it up to three times) for how they feel about the target words. After you ask how they feel, remember to always ask why they feel that way (metacognition).

Step by Step

1. Give a series of directions that use the vocabulary words you wish to review. For example:

   - "Clap once if *there is no way you would like* to be a **dictator**."
   - "Clap twice if *you think you might like* to be a **dictator**."
   - "Clap three times if *you would definitely like* to be a **dictator**."

   - "Clap once if *there is no way you would like* to be described as **lachrymose**."
   - "Clap twice if *you think you might like* to be described as **lachrymose**."
   - "Clap three times if *you would definitely like* to be described as **lachrymose**."

2. Another variation is to have students clap their thinking about a term and then get in groups with at least one other person who feels the same way (or a different way) to discuss why they feel the way they do. Explaining their thinking to each other helps students better understand the new terms or concepts (and argue with each other—which is not only something they love to do, but something that has the benefit of helping them remember the words).

Strategy 33

Mobile Meanings

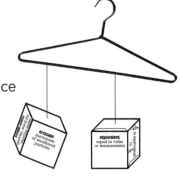

Making a vocabulary mobile is a hands-on learning experience that gives students an opportunity to demonstrate how much they know and understand about critical terms, ideas, events, or processes. I like to give students a wide variety of prompts when they make their cubes because you never know which prompts will light a spark for individuals. Sometimes the students I don't expect to choose the higher-level prompts do—and their work is amazing. This strategy uses a graphic pattern that becomes a foldable tool for vocabulary study.

Step by Step

1. Give students a pattern for a cube. The pattern is in the appendix labeled Strategy 33. You can write tasks on the cube before making student copies or give students a list of selections from which to choose.

2. Give prompts for tasks of varying complexity levels. This helps differentiate the learning in the activity. Students can choose from a range of tasks. The prompts you give will, of course, be tailored to the word or concept.

3. Students follow instructions to create a 3-D cube out of heavy paper, foam board, or poster board.

4. Students complete the six tasks on the faces of the cube. At least one of the faces must include the word and a definition or description.

   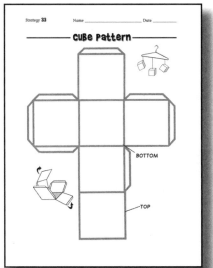

   Sample tasks:
   - Describe it or define it.
   - Compare it or give an example or synonym.
   - Contrast it or give a nonexample or antonym.
   - Illustrate it.
   - Analyze it.
   - Apply it.
   - Argue for or against it.
   - Create an analogy.
   - Create a pun.
   - Associate it with something personal that we have studied that it reminds you of, or connect it with something in your personal life.

5. After students complete the tasks, they fold and tape or glue the tabs to finish the cubes. Then, hang the various vocabulary cubes in a mobile form to display in the classroom. Students can explain their thinking to the class (*metacognition*).

Greet and Go

Greet and Go is an interactive activity to get students to use their prior knowledge to make predictions about what they are going to read and to set purposes for reading the text. It is a great way to preteach vocabulary. Students can complete the activity using the graphic organizer for Strategy 34.

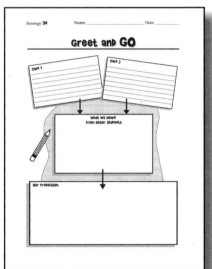

Step by Step

1. Prepare index cards for students. On each one write a different phrase or sentence from a text students are about to read.

2. Assign students to pairs. Give each student one of the prepared cards.

3. Students circulate around the room and read their cards to each other. They must be good listeners (a difficult thing for many students), and may not take notes. The idea is for them to pick up information from each other's passages and put it together to get an idea about the upcoming reading.

4. After a few minutes, have students return to their groups. Give each pair a copy of the graphic organizer for Strategy 34. Students quickly copy or summarize the phrase, sentence, or short passage that each of them bring to the mix. They add ideas they heard from other students. Finally, they use the information from their cards and from what they heard to jointly write a prediction of what the text passage will be about.

5. After reading the passage, they can check and discuss how their predictions relate to the passage itself.

How to Teach Academic Vocabulary
©Copyright Incentive Publications, Inc., Nashville, TN

In the Fast Lane

This is a quick and easy review activity to increase automaticity (being able to quickly recall and use words correctly). It deepens students' understanding of the target terms and takes only five to ten minutes of class time. You can use the graphic organizer for students to jot answers and help the race-car words hurry to the finish line.

Step by Step

1. List on the board or a projectable surface words that students should know. (The number will depend on the level of students and the focus of the lesson.)

2. Tell students that this activity will find out how much they know about the words. Explain that you will ask questions about the words and that you want students to answer quickly.

3. Ask a variety of questions about the word list—questions that will help students think about how the terms can be used or explained (metacognition), and get quick responses from the students. The kinds of questions will vary with your purposes, depending on what you want students to know. Here are some sample questions:

   • "Find me a word that can be both a noun and a verb."
   • "Find two adjectives (or other parts of speech) in our list."
   • "Find a word with a positive meaning."
   • "What does _____ mean?"
   • "How are _____ and _____ related?"
   • "Find two words with prefixes (suffixes)."
   • "Give me another form of _____."
   • "Find me a word that has to do with _____."
   • "Find me a word with two (or three) meanings."
   • "Show how you _____."
   • "Which word names an action? Show that action."

Alternative Approach

1. Make a copy of the graphic organizer for Strategy 35.

2. Present questions orally, giving each question a number.

3. Instead of answering orally, students individually or in pairs jot down answers on the racetrack in the lane corresponding to the question number. *(For example: If Question 1 is "Give me another form of "charity," students write the word "charity" first, then write another form of the word in Track 1.*

4. Students can share their answers with other groups or the whole class.

Finish This!

This is another easy strategy that fosters the association of new words or concepts with prior knowledge. The activity requires students to finish a sentence stem or complete an idea that the teacher begins. Completing these thoughts helps students understand that the new words can fit in their own vocabularies. The teacher structures the sentences with a question or sentence stem that requires students to integrate what they know and understand about the word's meaning in context to explain a situation. Such structure helps students avoid common errors in their thinking. After new words are introduced, the teacher uses them in a variety of instructions or questions that push students to think of a way that they have been involved with the action, event, condition, place, or idea named by the new word.

Step by Step

To help students connect the new words to their own experience, ask them to finish sentence stems or complete such ideas as these:

1. A time when I might **implicate** someone is _____.

2. Perhaps I would **ostracize** another person when _____.

3. _____ is a situation in which I would consider **abdicating**.

4. The tennis instructor said Sharon was a **novice** at the game because_____.

5. The banker was considered a **philanthropist** because_____.

6. What is something you could do to **impress** your teacher?_____.

7. Which of these things might be **extraordinary**: a person who has a library card or a person who has read all the books in the library?_____.

8. Say the word **clutch** if I mention something that you could clutch.
   (*Teacher says things like: purse, wallet, botulism, branches when you're climbing a tree, avarice, bumblebee.*)

9. Comparing Terms

   Alike (compare)

   _____ and _____ are similar because they both _____

   _____ .

   Different (contrast)

   _____ and _____ are different because _____

   is _____ but

   _____ is _____ .

Connotation Step-Up

This strategy gives students a visual model for stepping beyond the literal definition (denotation) or words to consider the broader implications or ideas that surround the particular thing, action, event, or condition named by the word. Students clarify the word definitions and then brainstorm with others to identify the connotations of the word. After they record ideas about connotations, they can start a lively discussion by comparing denotations and connotations. It is also interesting to illustrate the word and then discuss whether the illustration involves a strict denotation, the connotation, or both.

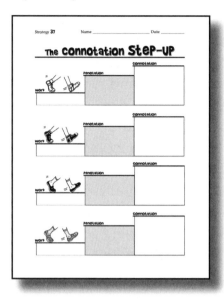

Step by Step

1. Prepare a list of words that you want students to explore.

2. Give students copies of the graphic organizer for Strategy 37.

3. Assign students a few words to write in the "Word" portion of the organizer.

4. Assist students with finding denotations for their words.

5. Let them work with a partner to write other words, phrases, or short sentences that describe the connotation of each word.

Strategy 38

Loop-de-Loop Game

The **Loop-de-Loop Game** is wonderful for strengthening vocabulary but it can easily be used for many other learning tasks (to review what has been learned and to check for understanding). I've found that once you start using looping cards, you come up with a variety of ways to use them. By using looping cards, students become actively involved in the learning and they must pay attention and listen to each card being read. Teachers can differentiate instruction by using multi-level looping activities. I prefer to make my own vocabulary looping cards, laminating them so I can use them over and over and keep them forever—since critical content vocabulary does not change!

Occasionally I'll let students make their own looping cards as a summative assessment, and they think it's great because they don't have a written test. They don't even realize how much they have to know to be able to get them done. (If they don't understand the terms or concepts, they can't make the cards.) I've seen students who would never study for a test work themselves to the bone getting their cards done. (I love it when activities make the kids work hard and have to think, and they don't even know it!)

Step by Step

1. Using small index cards or sturdy paper, create a card for each student that includes the following:

   • At the top of each card there is a statement that says, "I have . . ."

   • At the bottom of each card there is a question, "Who has . . ."

   • The first card is labeled "Start" at the top so the student with this card knows to begin the looping. The student with the "Start" card only reads the "Who has . . . ?" part of the card to begin the game. The last card says "Stop" at the bottom so the student with this card knows that the activity ends when his or her question is answered.

2. As an alternative to index cards, copy the looping cards pattern for Strategy 38 in the quantity you need and fill in the details for the cards

   Sample Looping Cards: *I have mixed up content to make my example. I want to make sure that all content-area teachers know that you can use this wonderful strategy in any content! Note that the START card answers the final question on the STOP card.*

Variation of Loop-de-Loop Game

This approach reverses the task. Instead of starting with the vocabulary word, concept, or equation, the reader starts with the definition for a word or concept or problem that is on another card.

Step by Step

1. Create a set of cards or strips that have a vocabulary word, concept, or equation or other problem with a definition or answer. (The definition or answer is for an item on another card.)

2. The first person who begins the looping reads the definition or answer (not the word), saying "Who has . . .", and the person with the word being defined says "I have . . ." and then reads the definition.

3. Continue until it loops back around to the first person.

4. Visit a Learning Loop Generator website: www.curriculumproject.com

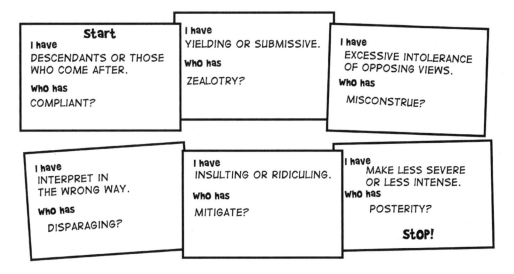

Vocabulary Dominoes

Vocabulary Dominoes is a game similar to the looping game. This strategy is a game that requires students to identify and review content vocabulary. Many students relate to dominoes and like to use them. You can write the information on the dominoes, and students can cut them out and match meanings to words. The activity becomes a hands-on, manipulative experience. Students can create the domino sequence by writing in words and meanings (or synonyms). OR, students can create the domino sets themselves by writing a "chain" on the graphic organizer. If they wish, they can cut out the dominoes, put them in an envelope, and share them with another student—turning the process into a fun game.

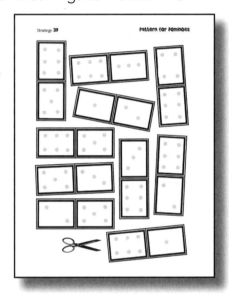

Step by Step

1. Copy the graphic page for Strategy 39 onto card stock. Make sets of dominoes, each domino having a word on one end and a definition for a different word on the other end. Be sure to label one end of the first domino, "START." The other dominoes should create a chain of words and definitions until the "END" domino.

2. Cut out the dominoes and put each set in an envelope. (Or enlist students to help cut out the dominoes.)

3. Students connect the cards by matching the words with their definitions.

4. This can be a timed activity. Pairs of students can compete against each other or against their previous time.

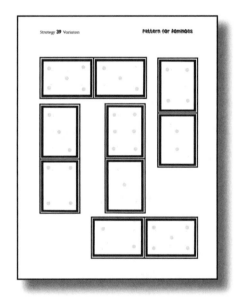

How to Teach Academic Vocabulary

In Your Own Words

Paraphrasing is very effective in helping students gain a better understanding of new terms, ideas, or concepts. The process of paraphrasing requires students to think about difficult text as they attempt to restate something in their own words. This activity uses a graphic organizer to guide students as they read a short text and show their understanding by putting it into their own words. When teaching this strategy, begin with a short piece of text and have students practice with a partner several times before they work alone.

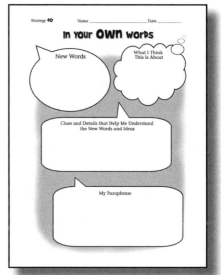

Step by Step

1. Give students copies of the graphic organizer for Strategy 40.

Before they read:

2. Students preview the text and identify new words from headings, boldfaced words, captions, or graphics.

3. From the preview, they predict what the passage will be about.

As they read:

4. Students read the text around the new words or ideas and write down any questions or ideas they get from the reading.

After they read:

After reading, students ask themselves some questions to help them understand the new terms. They note their answers in the appropriate talk balloons on the organizer.

5. Finally, students use the notes they have taken to help them paraphrase the text.

All Sorts of Sorts

Sorting requires students to make choices about how words should be classified or categorized. In addition, sorts involve active manipulation of the content, using the mind-body connection that helps concepts become part of long-term memory. Give students varied experiences with sorts, choosing the kinds that fit your content, your students' needs, and your purposes.

The graphic organizer provided for this strategy (labeled Strategy 41) leads students to sort words from their units, lessons, or content area by common word parts.

Sorts have many purposes:

- Sorts enable students to look at the structure of words in print as they examine the patterns in each word to determine how to categorize it.

- Students learn classification skills as they discover how sets of words, ideas, or concepts are alike or different.

- Sorts allow teachers to assess each student's understanding of what is being taught.

- Sorts are easy-to-check assessment tools that enable a teacher to evaluate a student's understanding of content quickly without the usual paper-pencil format.

- Sorts provide a multisensory experience as students read, sort, manipulate, and categorize in multiple ways.

- Sorts allow students to look at words, concepts, and ideas from their various levels of knowledge.

- Students are able to apply what they know in an organized and fun format.

- Students are empowered to make their own decisions about categories based on their prior knowledge.

SORTS are useful for vocabulary, comprehension, introducing a topic or concept, reviewing for a test—nearly everything!

Different Types of Sorts:

1. **Open sort**
   The teacher provides only the words, and students decide the sort categories based on what they see. Open sorts are valuable because they allow the teacher to see what students know and understand. Open sorts also allow for outside-the-box thinking.

2. Closed sort

The teacher provides the categories for the sort. Closed sorts are used more frequently than open sorts because they allow the teacher to focus the students' attention on a feature, characteristic, pattern, or concept that the class is studying. Closed sorts are also valuable assessment tools because the teacher can rapidly assess student understanding by checking the students' sorts for correctness.

3. Speed sort

This is usually a timed sort that students can do once they are adept at sorting. Speed sorts are excellent for building fluency and accuracy when working with well-known patterns and concepts. Students can record the time it takes to sort and then try to beat their own records.

4. Blind sort

This is a closed sort in which the teacher calls out the words and the students point to or say the categories they see listed on the worksheet, board, or overhead. Blind sorts are useful when the teacher wants to focus on sound patterns rather than visual patterns.

5. Writing sort

The students have key words written as column headers. They write words under the appropriate categories as the teacher calls them out, using the key words as spelling guides. Writing sorts focus on auditory and visual patterns in words and are a combination of closed and blind sorts.

Sample Criteria for Sorts:

- Word–Definition
- Word–Synonym (or Antonym)
- Questions–Answers
- Cause–Effect
- Problem–Solution
- Alike–Different
- Example–Nonexample
- Alphabetically
- Chronologically
- Numerically
- Meaning
- Form or Function

Step by Step

1. Determine the purpose of the sort.

2. Write letters, words, formulas, concepts, or problems on index cards or strips of paper. The number you use depends on grade level.

3. Place sorts in resealable plastic bags or envelopes. (This allows you to use them over and over.)

4. Students separate, categorize, or match cards depending on the criteria you give.

5. Have students work in pairs or individually.

6. As an alternative, create a graphic organizer such as the one used for word parts and have students identify words with those parts.

Try a sort on word parts.

The graphic organizer labeled *Strategy 41* uses the following 30 root words, prefixes, and suffixes. Brown and Cazden (1965) point out that these root words, prefixes, and suffixes provide the basis for more than 14,000 commonly used words in the English language.

When you create a Word-Part Sort for your subject area, make sure you include these content-related word parts:

Math:	bi, circum, dia, iso, mono, multi, per, peri, poly, quad, semi, super, tetra, trans, tri, uni, penta, octo/octa, deca, hexa, nona, cent
Health/Science:	ab, co, con, demi, dia, dys, epi, hetero, homo, hydro, hyper, hypo, infra, meta, micro, neo, para, per, peri, proto, photo, sub, trans, via, ology
Social Studies:	ab, ad, anti, arch, at, con, contra, countr, demi, epi, ethno, ex, il, im, multi, neo, ob, omni, para, poly, pro, trans, via, vice

Strategy 42

3 Facts + 1 Fib Game

This activity gives students a chance to review and process content from the text in a fun, interactive way. It is important to model and practice this first. Students sometimes find it hard to remember that what they want to do is fool or trick as many of the other students as they can with their false statements about the vocabulary term, concept, or process.

The graphic organizer can help students organize their thoughts ahead of time.

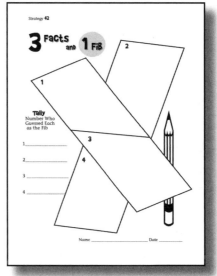

Step by Step

1. After students learn new terms (or concepts or processes) ask them to choose one of the terms (or concepts or processes) that represents critical information all students should know and understand. Individuals may make different choices. This is to be encouraged!

2. Give students copies of the graphic organizer for Strategy 42.

3. Explain to students that they will think of four statements about the word, concept, or process—statements that reflect on what it means. Three of these statements should be true, and one should be false. Remind them that the game will be to share these with other students for the purpose of seeing if students really understand the word or idea.

4. Students circulate around the room and show their lists of statements to at least five other students. The other students try to identify which statement is the "fib."

5. With some practice, students will learn to be "crafty" so that the "fibs" sound as much like the truth as possible. They might also learn to write the "facts" in a way that requires that others thoroughly understand the term or concept in order not to be misled into thinking that one of the "facts" might be a "fib."

Strategy 43

On Target!

Structured Word Associations

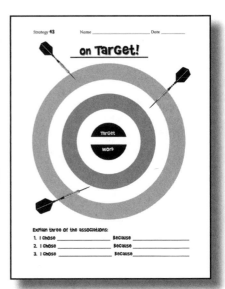

In this type of activity, the teacher gives student-friendly definitions of the new (target) words and then scaffolds the learning by using words that students already know to help them understand the meanings of the new words. Once the target word is introduced, students are asked to associate it with a presented word or phrase. Associating a known word with a newly learned word further reinforces the meaning of the new word. For example, a teacher may have students associate the new word *novice* with the word *kindergartner*. Because individuals will make associations different from one another, it is critical that you ask students to explain why they chose the connection they made. Explaining their thinking (metacognition) helps students process information and mentally manipulate it. Graphic organizers such as **On Target!** and **Follow the Clues** can assist the word associations.

Not all word associations have to be structured. Here are some other ways that teachers can teach word associations in less structured ways.

Step by Step

Free Word Association

This is a quick and unstructured way to review vocabulary. Students are asked to give the words they think of when the teacher gives a particular term.

A-B Pairing

1. Students are grouped in pairs. One student is designated as A and one is B. (You can use numbers, colors, animals, or anything you choose for the labeling of students.)

2. The teacher calls out target terms (such as: *measurement, collinear, technology*).

3. While student B listens, student A talks nonstop, responding with words that come to mind when he or she hears the target words.

4. Then students reverse roles. Student B talks nonstop and student A listens. B cannot repeat anything said by A but can expand on what A has said.

Oral Word Association

The teacher calls out a target term or concept.

1. Students take turns (as a class, in small groups, or in pairs) saying any word they think that is related to the target term.

How to Teach Academic Vocabulary
©Copyright Incentive Publications, Inc., Nashville, TN

2. After a few minutes, the teacher says, "Stop." The last person to say a word must explain how that word is related to the target word.

3. To ensure that students pay attention to one another's responses, require that they repeat the previous response before offering their own.

4. Another way to ensure that students listen to others is to use the graphic organizer for Strategy 43 as a place for them to record what they hear. Students working as partners take turns saying any word related to the target term. Students write others' words on the target (not their own). After the teacher stops them, they choose words from the target and ask the partner to explain his or her thinking when the association was made.

On Target (Written Word Association)

1. Give students copies of the graphic organizer for Strategy 43.

2. Students write their responses to the target term or concept. (Ask, "What other words or phrases come to your mind when you hear the word . . . .?")

3. When you say, "Stop," students take time to explain three of the associations they made. They write these explanations in the allotted space on the organizer.

4. Then students exchange papers with a partner. First, partners read what the other person wrote in the way of explanation at the bottom of the organizer. Then they can ask each other to explain any of the other words on their lists.

Follow the Clues! (Verbal-Visual Word Association)

This variation of word associations is for those of you who like to use graphic organizers. Notice that the target learning here is a root, prefix, or suffix, but students must make associations with a word that uses the target word part. This helps students clarify and develop an understanding about word parts. You can use the same process with any vocabulary term or important concept. Students write and show words they know that contain the word part you want them to learn.

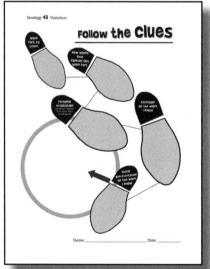

1. Give students copies of the graphic organizer labeled Strategy 43, Variation

2. Students write a root, prefix, or suffix that you want them to learn. They follow the footsteps to relate this new word part to words they know, and add new words that use the part.

3. They repeat the process with other words that include the root, prefix, or suffix. Or you can give different word parts to different students. Then students can share their work, exposing them to several different word parts in one lesson.

Words on a Wall

Most teachers are familiar with Word Walls. It is important to note that effective Word Walls are not cute posters, lists of words, decorations, or the letters of the alphabet. They are intentional attempts to use the power of visualization as a learning strategy to increase long-term memory for students. The idea is to present words, concepts written briefly, formulas, or other content that students need to learn, review, and remember. Words are placed on a wall when the teacher intends to use them as a part of lessons or review. Many games and active lessons can be built around the Word Wall.

Step by Step

1. Generate a list of essential words, concepts, formulas, or whatever is critical for students to know and remember in your content. Include only essential information.

2. Add words or other items of information gradually. (Do not let the Word Wall become overcluttered.)

3. Practice and refer to the word or information every time it is discussed or used. Emphasize frequently the information and how it can be used—before, during, and after the lesson. Use specific, planned activities such as those listed below.

4. Once the word information is a part of the learning wall, expect students to spell and use the information correctly in their work.

5. Use the wall to create a chart (or format or list) for important information.

6. Try using the same color for words that share the same concept.

7. Change colors when the theme, chapter, or area of study changes. (Remember that the brain thinks in symbols, color, location, pattern, and odd numbers.)

8. Place the words or other information in a prominent place in your classroom. It doesn't have to be on the wall—you might try your windows, doors, or ceilings.

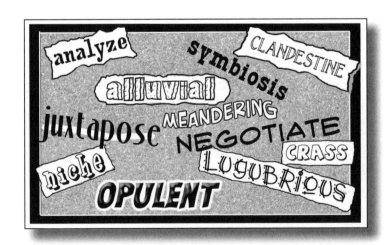

Word Wall Activities

Word Hunt

Look on the wall for particular words related to another word or concept, or matching given criteria.

Rivet

The teacher draws spaces for words and fills in one letter at a time until students recognize the word.

Memory

Cover the word wall and divide class into teams. Team members work together to see who can remember the most words in five minutes.

Partner Quiz

Randomly give out the letters of the alphabet. Student groups read and define all the words on the word wall that begin with that letter.

Read My Mind

Students number their papers 1 to 5. The teacher gives five clues for a particular word on the word wall. Students write down the word. They may keep the same word or change to a different word, as led by the clues. The winner is the student who chose the correct word on the earliest clue.

Telephone Game

The student at the head of each row chooses a word from the word wall and whispers the definition of the word in the ear of the next student. This student, in turn, whispers the heard definition to the next student. The definition is passed in this way until it reaches the last person. This person announces the definition heard and compares it with the correct definition.

Word Up!

Each student chooses a word from the word wall and completes the following to be shared with the class:

   Word   What it is   What it isn't   Synonym   Antonym   How it is used

Pass Along

Each student writes a simple phrase using a word from the wall. He or she then passes the paper to another student who adds another phrase using another wall word. That student passes the paper once more, adding another phrase containing a wall word and checking the sentence.

Communication Game

The teacher rolls a die. If the roll is 1 or 2, a student must act out a wall word. If the roll is 3 or 4, a student must draw, without talking, the word meaning for the class to guess. If the roll is 5 or 6, the student must explain the word without using the word itself or body motions.

Get Moving

Students spell wall words using their arms. Tall letters are spelled with arms straight up in the air. Small letters are spelled with arms bent and hands on hips. Dropped letters are spelled with hands on hips and knees bent.

Riddles, Riddles, Riddles

Students work in pairs to create a riddle for a word on the wall. The pairs take turns sharing riddles so the rest of the class can try to guess the word.

Roll That Die

Roll a die. Students identify words on the word wall having that number of letters, giving a definition and a sentence for each.

Word Wall Stories

Divide the class into teams. Each team writes a creative story using as many wall words as possible.

Crisscross Words

This is played like Scrabble, where students choose words and fit them together.

How Much Are Your Words Worth?

Students search the wall for words that add up to a certain predetermined value (*a = 1, b = 2, c = 3, and so on*).

20 Questions

Students take turns asking Yes or No questions about the word.

"I Spy"

Have students search the wall by saying, "I spy with my little eye, a word that . . . ." Complete it with a clue such as "is the antonym of *sad*" or "rhymes with *stop*" or "is a verb" or "means . . . ."

Scavenger Hunt

Students search the word wall for words that fit a certain category.

Alliterative Sentences

Students write a sentence using as many word wall words beginning with the same letter as possible.

Fix-It

Students identify words that have prefixes and suffixes.

Syllabicate

Students choose words to divide into syllables.

Sentences

Students choose a noun and a verb from the wall, then write declarative, interrogative, imperative, and exclamatory sentences using the two words.

Context Clues

Students write a sentence leaving a blank for a word wall word to be inserted.

Concentration Game

Games engage students in learning. And, when used properly, they serve as effective reinforcement and review for students. Students need the opportunity to demonstrate what they know in a variety of ways, and games provide a chance for all students to be successful. When playing the **Concentration** game, students have fun learning words in a game situation and find joy in learning content vocabulary.

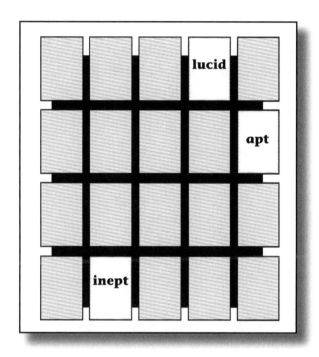

Step by Step

1. Prepare a set of ten matching cards (word and definition, antonyms, synonyms, compound words).

2. Lay all cards face down.

3. Player 1 picks up two cards at a time.

4. If the two cards match, Player 1 keeps the cards. If the two cards do not match, the player puts the cards face down, back in the same position.

5. The game proceeds until all matches are made.

Name That Category!

This game helps students focus on the attributes of concepts represented or associated with terms as they try to determine what a group of terms have in common (modeled after *The $20,000 Pyramid*). Work with categories that are a part of a lesson, unit, or big idea you have studied with your students. The graphic organizer for Strategy 46 can be used as a part of the game.

Step by Step

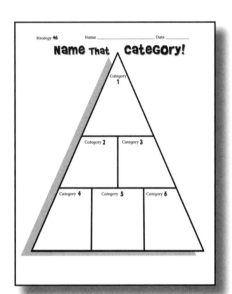

1. Make a copy of the triangular (pyramid outline) graphic organizer labeled Strategy 46 or create a triangular game board divided into six cells (sections)—three on the bottom, two in the middle, and one on the top. (This can be on overhead transparency, white board, poster board, or a computer-generated template.)

2. Write a category name on each cell, increasing the level of difficulty as you move through the categories. Hide the category names before the game begins. (When using the graphic organizer, do not write anything on the organizer ahead of time.)

3. Assign students to work in pairs or small groups. One player on each team is the clue giver and should be able to see the game board. All others, the guessers, must keep their backs to the game board. (If you are using the graphic organizer, whisper the category to the one player on each team who will be the clue giver.

4. The clue giver, who sees one category at a time on the game board or has had the category whispered to him or her, starts listing words that fit that category and continues until teammates correctly identify the category name.

5. Reveal the next category as soon as a team correctly identifies the first category.

6. When a team has guessed all categories, they should raise their hands and shout, "Got it!" This is a clue for all teams to stop.

Roll-A-Word

Roll-A-Word is a dice game that helps students make words using base words, roots, prefixes, and suffixes. Make sure the word parts you select for the game create words from your content.

Step by Step

1. Groups of three or four students will take turns rolling a die. Each person in the group rolls the die three times at each turn. The number on the die determines each of the following:

   • first roll determines the prefix

   • second roll determines the base word or root

   • third roll determines the suffix

2. As a group, students make as many words as possible each time a team member rolls. Words must have at least two of the word parts in them.

3. Students write the words in a list and take turns rolling the die in the time allowed. (The words must be "real" words.)

4. The group with the most words wins.

Prefix	Base word/root	Suffix
1 in, ir	1 form—shape	1 ent, ant
2 de	2 port—carry	2 ism
3 uni	3 tract—draw or pull	3 ness
4 con	4 cred—believe	4 er, or
5 trans	5 duct—lead	5 able, ible
6 re	6 aud—to hear	6 ess

Snap-Crackle-Pop! Game

This game can be the centerpiece for a learning station or it can be used as a whole-class activity at the end of a unit. I take index cards, cut them into strips, and write one vocabulary term, event, person, or important concept on each strip for the game. Also include three additional strips—one that says "SNAP," one that says "CRACKLE," and one that says "POP." These are the wild cards in the game. Give each team one answer sheet with all the terms and definitions and a set of the cards you have made.

Not to be obnoxious, but this means that you'll need five sets of cards if you have five teams! I just want you to know that you'll need to prepare ahead of time for this game.

Step by Step

1. Each team is given a container holding the words for the game. *I use baskets, but you can use anything that will hold the strips.*

2. The students (or you) designate one person in each group (or team) to be the leader. Only that leader sees cards that are drawn and knows the correct answers. The leader will hold the answer sheet during the game and will not show it to anyone.

3. Starting with the person on the leader's right, each person takes turns drawing a card out of the container. The person drawing the card does not look at it, but hands it to the leader.

4. The leader reads the clue, question, word, or definition from the answer sheet to the person. If the person gets the answer right, he or she gets to keep the card. If the answer is wrong, the card goes back into the container, the leader mixes up the cards, and the next person takes a turn.

How to Teach Academic Vocabulary

5. If someone draws a Snap, Crackle, or Pop card, all of their accumulated cards go back in the container. The Snap, Crackle, or Pop card DOES NOT go back into the basket. There is only one of each word in the container, so there can be only three bad draws during a game.

6. The game is over when all the cards are gone from the container or when time is called.

7. The winner is the person with the most cards. How about a Rice Krispies Treat as the award for the winner?

> *Note: This idea can be adapted to become a vocabulary station to help students review standardized test terms (verbs from your standards), roots and affixes, content-specific vocabulary, or just about anything you want them to learn. I've included a general list of standardized test terms that students might see on state tests, so you could get an idea of how I do it. You would need to select the terms and definitions that fit with your state test. Because these are not easy terms, I reverse the process—putting the definitions into the basket. Then students have to name the term that matches the definition.*

Standardized Test Terms and Definitions

Analyze	To break down into its parts or subparts; to examine critically
Apply	To use, often in a new situation; to look at the relevance
Argue	To use logic and evidence to prove truth or action
Assess	To estimate the value or importance of
Cause and Effect	To explain the reason for something and the results or consequence of that event
Change	To alter, replace, or modify something
Compare	To note the similarities or resemblances; to explain something complex by analogy to some more familiar object or term
Compose	To put things together in a creative way
Conclude	To decide or determine something from the evidence; to infer or deduce from the facts or evidence
Construct	To make or build something
Contrast	To use evidence to show differences; to compare the dissimilarities
Create	To give rise to or originate something new
Criticize	To judge or decide the worth
Decide	To settle or determine an issue; to choose or make up one's mind
Defend	To uphold a position with evidence or facts
Define	To clarify or explain the meaning of a term, idea, etc.
Demonstrate	To describe or explain by giving examples
Describe	To represent by words and/or pictures
Elaborate	To expand an idea or issue with full details and care
Estimate	To form an opinion or judgment from what you are given
Evaluate	To decide on the value of an idea or topic from the evidence
Expand	To add to the information already given; to add more to a statement
Explain	To prove a point with specific reason
Identify	To give a name, classification, or description; to make something recognizable or understandable
Illustrate	To make something clear by giving examples, drawings, etc.
Infer	To come to a decision or conclusion based on the evidence; to make an assumption based on what facts you have been given
Interpret	To show the meaning; to explain or translate
Persuade	To convince the audience, in writing or speech, that your ideas, points, arguments or evidence should be accepted
Predict	To make a guess or decision based on information that is given to you

Vocabulary Hip-Hop

The pairing of skills or concepts with music or rhythm is a great brain-compatible learning strategy. When students sing, dance, or tap out rhythm along with lyrics that define words or explain a concept, the brain will repeat the concepts and put them into long-term memory. In addition, the rhythm and movement that accompany the music motivate students to participate in the learning experience! When the students actually create the song or rap themselves, the learning is further deepened. So look for opportunities to engage students in writing verses of poetry, song lyrics, or rap.

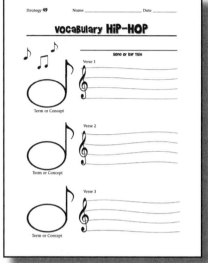

Enjoy the example on the next page ("The MMMR Rap") and share it with your students. Then use the graphic organizer for Strategy 49 as a guide for students to strengthen word meanings or concepts in your content area by writing their own hip-hop or rap songs.

Step by Step

1. Share short poems, songs, or raps that others have written to explain a term or concept. (Use the following rap as an example, or make up a few simple ones of your own.)

2. Identify key terms or concepts from a lesson or unit that students need to understand. Make a list of these available for students.

3. Take one term or idea and work with students to develop a short rap. (Use the graphic organizer for Strategy 49.)

4. Divide students into pairs or groups of three. Give each group one or two terms (or concepts) that they will "explain" through the medium of a hip-hop song or rap. Remind them that their purpose is to teach the term or concept to other students or to help themselves know and remember the term well.

5. Give groups copies of the graphic organizer for Strategy 49 as a guide for their work.

6. If the words that are being defined focus on a unified theme, each small group can work on one verse. Then the verses can be combined into a larger piece.

Note: The RAP on the following page was developed by Connie Thomason, Co-Teacher, College Hill Middle School in Texarkana, Arkansas. (Co-teaching involves one special ed teacher and one regular ed teacher working together.) Connie says: "I use Cultural Proficiency as a tool to guide my lessons and make a personal connection with students. I developed this RAP and paired it with an interactive PowerPoint to energize even the most reluctant learner. My students beg for more as I provide motivational and high-impact lessons that address different modalities of learning. By getting the students actively involved, I have fewer discipline problems and more parental involvement.

Name _____ Date _____

MMMR Rap

Boys and girls listen up-
It's a word from the wise.
I got a quick lesson
That won't cost you a dime

Mode, Mean, Median
It won't go away.
So open up your minds-
Cause this is the day.

MODE means MOST
This number is greedy.
It appears more
Than any other lil' seedlings.

MEDIAN means MIDDLE
When you're driving down the road.
Don't look away-
Or your car will explode.

Looking for the middle
Is quite easy to do.
From smallest to largest
List triples and twos.

Time to start slashing-
Go from left to right.
The man in the middle
Won't put up a fight.

Two men left
What should I do?
Push plus on the calculator
And divide by two.

Time for the finale
By all **MEANS** -
Let's look at the size
Of your jeans.

We got a 30, 30, 36, 42
Oh my gosh-
What should I do?

Let's add them all together
And don't you forget.
Divide by four
Before you hit the reset.

Last but not least
Is our friend the **RANGE.**
Not hard to learn-
Just a little strange.

Start with the high
And subtract from the low
Now you got the RAP
And there is NO MO!

Developed by
Connie Thomason,
Texarkana, Arkansas, 2008,
and used with permission.

Vocabulary-O

The good old standby game of Bingo can be used to sharpen skills and understandings in many categories and many content areas. This one can be used for a variety of vocabulary activities. Start with a list of words that students have learned. Then use the game to strengthen understanding of any characteristics you choose. The graphic organizer offers a basic format for playing the **Vocabulary-O** game.

Step by Step

1. Prepare a list of about 30 words for which you want students to reinforce meanings or deepen understandings. (These may be review words from a unit of study.) Give students copies of this list.

2. Give each student a copy of the graphic organizer with the Vocabulary-O board.

3. Students prepare their boards by writing one term from the list in each block. Tell them to mix up the terms (not write them in order). They will have to make choices, because the list will have more words than the board has spaces.

4. Make sure each student has a set of items to use as markers on the board. These can be pennies, paper markers, plastic dots, kernels of popcorn, or anything else you choose.

5. Decide what approach you will take for the Vocabulary-O game. When the game is played, you will be giving clues. Students will place their markers on a word that matches your clues. Your clue can be the definition, a synonym, an antonym, a part of speech, or a word part with its meaning. For example, your clues might be something like one of the following:

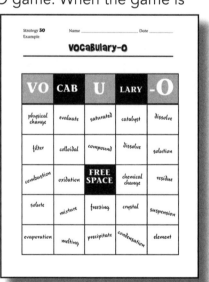

   - Find a word that names a scientific process.
   - Find a word that is a synonym for **scrutinize**.
   - Find a word that has a suffix meaning **one who**.
   - Find a word that is an antonym for **durable**.
   - Find a word that describes the type of government in which a king or queen rules the country.
   - What literary device is used in this sentence?
     The toaster shot out its fiery tongue and grabbed my toast.
   - Find a word that names an element in this equation: $6x + y^2 = 33$

6. As in the game of Bingo, students place markers on words that match the clues or answer the questions. When a student has a solid row of markers (horizontal, diagonal, or vertical) he or she hollers out, "VOCABULARY-O!" Students must justify their choices.

Chapter 4

Teaching the Strategies, Activities, and Games

*" Whether you think you can,
or whether you think you can't,
you're right."*

– Henry Ford

Teach One Strategy at a Time

I've got to be honest and tell you that if teachers focus on helping students learn academic vocabulary to increase their content comprehension, that means that many teachers are going to have to rethink what they are currently doing in the classroom. Students need time and practice to learn academic vocabulary (or any other content) well. It takes preparation and effort by teachers to figure out how teaching vocabulary strategies can be incorporated into daily lessons. Most teachers already feel overwhelmed by the amount of content they need to cover. Learning new vocabulary strategies is one more thing to teach. If students are going to internalize the instruction and be able to use strategies independently, they need time to review and practice the strategies using activities and games. How can all of this be accomplished when many teachers feel tied to their textbooks and pressured by state standards and tests?

The best way to start anything new or different is to take it step by step. Just like we need to stop and decide what is most important for our students to know and understand to be successful, we need to stop and think about how we teach and what is or isn't working. I realized that my students could memorize words and definitions like crazy, but two weeks after the test, they acted like they'd never seen the words in their lives. I knew I needed to do something differently, or I'd be reteaching and reviewing the same words the whole year! After reading all the research and as many books as I could, I decided to tackle teaching vocabulary in a different way, and here is what worked for me.

I pick one vocabulary strategy, activity, or game each grading period that I use consistently—so the kids can really learn it. This approach works even better if you can get a grade level, team, or subject area team to determine the strategies all the teachers will focus on.

Make a plan. What a unique idea! I wonder if this is what they mean by a Professional Learning Community, PLC.

This way kids learn the strategies in a variety of content areas from more than one teacher; and they can actually make the connection that this strategy will help them in more than one class. Imagine—helping kids make connections among the content areas!

Doing strategies this way does not mean that teachers are limited in the other strategies they use; it simply means that there is a focus on

How to Teach Academic Vocabulary

one strategy at a time so that kids will learn using a variety of teaching styles and in a variety of content areas.

Too often we get excited about doing too many new things at once and we don't take the time to see if they really help the kids or if they are just the "idea of the day."

Teachers must continue to incorporate the learned strategy throughout the year as they teach students other strategies. Identifying focus strategies allows teachers to teach a number of strategies thoroughly, avoiding a hit-and-miss approach with multiple strategies. If the school were to make a plan for strategies that all students will learn at each grade level, think about the number of vocabulary strategies students could really know and understand when they leave the school!

Remember that the strategies themselves are not sacred. Take the ones (or parts of ones) that work best for your content or grade level and make them your own!

I like to combine direct instruction with a variety of other ideas about how students learn best.

The Instructional Steps for Effective Vocabulary Instruction

When I teach important words that are critical to the understanding of the lesson, I use the same steps every time so students know the teaching routine. Once they learn the routine, they know what to expect and begin to take on more responsibility for their own learning. I consciously try to use the steps for systematic and explicit instruction discussed in Chapter 2.

Whenever I teach a vocabulary strategy, I follow this set of steps:

- Hook the students and give them a clear and concise description of the strategy—when to use it and how it should be used.
- Model the strategy for the students. (ME)
- Repeat the strategy, this time enlisting the students' help. (WE)
- Give students the opportunity to use the strategy in pairs—a gradual release of responsibility for the learning from the teacher to the students. (TWO)
- Give students opportunities to use the strategy independently. (YOU)

Systematic and Explicit Instruction for Academic Vocabulary

Once my students understand the ME, WE, TWO, YOU process, I use another systematic and explicit routine to teach individual vocabulary words. These are the steps I use in my vocabulary routine:

- Teacher uses a graphic organizer and gives student-friendly explanation of each new term. Students repeat each term aloud.
- Students discuss terms in pairs.
- Students construct a picture, symbol, or graphic representation.
- Students create a vocabulary notebook; restate definition in their own words in writing and record picture, symbol, or graphic.
- Words are added to word wall/learning wall.
- Students engage in activities and refine definitions in vocabulary notebooks.
- Students play word games.

My Daily Vocabulary Routine

Even if I have 25 or 30 words that are important in the unit, I follow the same steps as I teach the strategy but I chunk the words into groups of five to seven and then teach those new words at the beginning of class each day. By Friday, students know all the words for the week, and I can give them a vocabulary test on Monday instead of Friday. My goal is to include auditory and mind-body connections to help students start retaining the new words in long-term memory. Here are the steps that have worked for me:

1. **Choose a graphic organizer**

   I like to use the hand organizer because it has five digits—a good number of words to chunk together. Also students have a hand attached to their bodies; they can't lose it, it goes everywhere with them, and they can use it as a prompt to think in my class!

   I have students hold up fingers starting with their pinkie and I tell them the new word and have them wiggle the finger. I then have them pronounce the word. I say it once more and then I tell them to say it. Depending on the difficulty of the word and the age group of the students, I might repeat the word and emphasize syllables. Then I have them do the word in syllables with me and finally, they say it again as one complete word.

   I do this same process with every finger, so remember, if you don't want kids shooting you the bird with their middle finger, you had better not use the hand organizer. Your best bet is to use a star, because it also has five points. I will tell you that my students tried to be funny and use the middle finger, but when I acted like it was normal and part of the learning process rather than something else, they got over it. It really won't matter what grade level you teach; all students love the idea of shooting the teacher the bird. I still have graduate students who will come up to me years later and use their middle finger to recall a word they learned in our class!

2. Explain the term in a way that relates to their prior knowledge. (Use kid-friendly terms.)

It is important for students to understand the new term in language that they know and understand. Sometimes I give synonyms or phrases they already know so they can make the connection to the new word. In other words, the second thing good teachers do is scaffold the learning! We go from what they know to the new word.

3. Give examples.

As part of the explanation of the new word, I give an example or two using the term so the kids will better understand the meaning. The examples don't have to be from the current lesson but they do have to be things that students recognize and can relate to in their own experience.

4. Have students work in pairs.

After we go over all five words and do the first three steps, I put students in pairs. One person takes the first three words on the graphic organizer and explains what each word means in his own words; then the second person takes the last two words and using his graphic organizer explains what those two words mean. When they finish, they work together to create a visual that would remind them of what the word means if they didn't have words they could use.

5. Share informally to assess learning.

After the students finish discussing their meanings of the words and creating their visuals, I ask for volunteers to share. The results of this informal sharing can be quite amazing. In most classes where there are such academically diverse learners, this allows students to gain a healthy respect for the different ways that we learn and remember new information. Many times students will like what another pair shares and will change their own definitions or visuals. It gives me the opportunity to check for misconceptions right away and know what I'll need to clarify as we use the words during the lesson.

Once you get good at these five steps, they take only 10 to 15 minutes at the beginning of class, and the effort is well worth it. Students start really remembering the important terms! I find kids using their hand graphic organizers (wiggling fingers) all through the year during tests to remember what words mean and how to use them. I must admit that I've gone so far as to use both hands and feet to teach 20 words, so there have been many times when my students are wiggling fingers and toes during lessons.

Other teachers ask me what my students were doing during state tests when this happened. I finally had to show the whole faculty the process, so they wouldn't think my students were cheating or that I was weird!

Vocabulary Discussions in the Classroom

For students to really internalize new learning, they need to have opportunities to share their ideas and thinking (metacognition). Many of our students are such auditory learners that they often must hear something said aloud in order to know if it makes sense. With this in mind, I like to include classroom discussions as part of how I teach academic vocabulary. It is just one more tool in my toolbox to help students learn new vocabulary and content. There are many ways to get students to discuss content, but I'm going to give you a few of my favorites. Notice that almost all of them build on the fact that students like to argue (they'll argue with a wall!) and challenge authority (they always want the last word).

- Challenge students' thinking of new vocabulary or concepts by helping them identify and debate opposing points of view. This can be done with directed questions that force students to clarify their thinking and positions and provoke meaningful discussions (arguments). You will know you are successful with this type of discussion when students are at enough at ease in this risk-free environment to feel comfortable challenging any position.

- Propose outcomes for hypothetical events or outcomes different from what actually happened. For instance, *"What if we didn't have . . . ? What if the war had been won by . . . ?"* The use of this technique provokes students to think beyond what they know about the words, and forces them to examine and reorganize the available information to develop deeper understanding of the terms.

- Have students rearrange a list of terms (for example, the stages of the water cycle) in some given order (from the most important to least important, least significant to most significant). Vary the technique by having students select

How to Teach Academic Vocabulary
©Copyright Incentive Publications, Inc., Nashville, TN

the three most important terms. From a list of scientific advances (atomic energy, improved breeding of farm animals, space travel) ask students to identify the two or three that have been most beneficial to man. Making selections based on their own criteria, actively discussing similarities and differences, and participating in any number of analytical exercises can help students deepen their understanding of the terms.

- Give students a number of opposing views with appropriate rationale for each. Students analyze each one and its merits. Students must provide evidence for their positions.

- Give an unfinished oral or written account and ask students to furnish conclusions. This approach is ideal for role-playing.

- Present students with a list of several problems and solutions. Students must select and defend solutions.

- Present students with a list of adjectives and ask which best characterize an event or person. This approach helps them understand stereotypes and generalizations.

Before, During, and After the Reading

Teaching academic vocabulary must be done before, during, and after the lesson depending on the teacher's purpose. Even after teachers introduce the words and use them in context with students, it takes multiple encounters with a word for students to actually learn it. Students come to class with many different levels of word knowledge, so strategies must fit a variety of levels at one time. Teachers must create ways that students can associate vocabulary with something meaningful so that students can do more than just memorize words, formulas, or concepts. Once these connections are made, it will be more likely that the new information will be remembered. After the new content is associated with meaning, use activities, games, and additional practice with the content. Provide visual, auditory, and kinesthetic ways for students to learn and remember content-specific vocabulary and concepts.

Students need to interact with key words in a variety of ways in a short period of time. We must include activities that will build their speaking and writing vocabularies (expressive) and their listening and reading vocabularies (receptive). As teachers select vocabulary strategies, activities, and games for their classrooms, they should remember that students require active learning, which, by definition, should involve more than traditional worksheets, word lists, multiple choice, and matching activities.

Before Reading

Before students read is the best time to teach vocabulary strategies that will help them understand the content. This is where consciously competent teachers decide, as experts, what best will help their students succeed. It is very tempting not to use this valuable time for teaching a strategy, because we want to cover the content; but taking the time up front is critical for long-term success. Follow these steps:

- Build background knowledge and purpose for the lesson.
- Preteach important terms or vocabulary.
- Relate new information to previously learned information.
- Interpret the visuals and the captions in the text (charts, graphics, maps, pictures).
- Go over the questions students are to answer, before they read.

During Reading

Reading and comprehending what they are reading is not an easy task for all students. If they do not understand the content-specific vocabulary, asking them to read the text silently and then answer questions or do a worksheet is not effective. As we rethink how we teach for understanding, try something different to get students actively involved in what they are reading. These ideas will not replace silent reading all the time, but if you use some of these techniques, more students will be able to read silently when it is the only option. Try these techniques:

- Pair students and have them read aloud to each other or in unison.
- Read aloud and have students follow along. At designated words or phrases, the teacher pauses and the students fill in the missing words.
- Call on one student to read, then have that student calls on the next person. Students have the right to pass and call on another person.
- Read aloud as one or more students echo what you have read using the same style and intonations.
- Pair students and have them read orally or silently; then take turns retelling the information in their own words. Partners should be told to elaborate or add any missing content.
- Have students keep learning logs or journals so they can think about what they understand or what they do not understand as they read (metacognition).
- Use chapter mapping, webs, and semantic feature analysis.

- Have students work in groups (socializing)—pairs, triads, cooperative learning, peer editing, paired reading, writing a commercial, producing a radio play, debate.
- Activate and use prior knowledge and reflect on new understanding.
- Help students set a purpose for reading.
- Model fix-up strategies—predict, clarify, reread the text, read on, question, and summarize.
- Read aloud to students from a variety of texts so they gain fluency in the content.
- Pause during in-class reading to have students predict.

After Reading

Teachers have always done most of the things listed here after students read in their classes. Unfortunately, because many of us didn't teach effectively before and during the reading, the after-reading performance of some students was often disappointing. If you use some of the ideas about teaching before and during the reading, you'll find more students will have success after reading. They'll understand more of the content and remember more of the essential vocabulary.

- Discuss the content and synthesize the concepts that were learned.
- Review the significant terms or vocabulary.
- Extend the lesson through writing, projects, or some other type of enrichment activity.
- Assign students to dramatize and perform brief skits.
- Have students create games based on reading.
- Have students assume the personae of characters and engage in a panel discussion.
- Have students create illustrated flash cards for vocabulary terms.
- After reading informational texts, ask five questions:
  1. Did you find the answers to our questions about what we were reading (or which questions did we find the answers to)?
  2. What questions didn't we find the answers to?
  3. What else did you learn that we didn't think about?
  4. What is the most surprising or interesting thing we read and learned?
  5. What do we now know that we didn't know before?

Some Final Thoughts on How We Teach Academic Vocabulary

I believe it is time to realize that much of what we are currently doing in our classrooms isn't as effective as we would like it to be. If you agree with that idea, then it is time to rethink and start using specific strategies, activities, and games to help students increase their academic vocabulary so they can better understand the content. Please understand I am not suggesting you add more teaching "stuff" to your already full plate. Students feel the same way about what they learn. If you're just adding more "stuff" for them to do and be tested on, then they will not understand the importance of learning strategies. Do the following to set yourself and your kids up for success:

- Motivating students to want to use the strategy is important. Give explanations, discuss the value of the strategy, and explain why it is important in real life. Don't test them on the strategy!

- Provide extended practice, encouragement, and feedback over a long period of time. Transfer of the learning to other situations (like state tests) is not automatic. It must be worked on continually.

- Students must learn to reflect on what they are learning, as well as how to use strategies in a variety of situations.

Teachers can foster vocabulary development by providing:

- Systematic and explicit instruction in new words and their meanings
- Repetition and multiple exposures to academic vocabulary
- Spontaneous instruction whenever the opportunity arises
- Experiences such as field trips that provide natural occasions for learning new words
- Enjoyable opportunities to listen to stories, videos, and tapes in which the new words are heard and learned
- An emphasis on word meaning, rather than on mechanical pronunciation
- Words in context rather than in isolation
- Opportunities to ask questions about any unusual or confusing words as they are encountered and for students who speak other languages to share their words, concepts, or idioms that relate to the words

"The mediocre teacher tells. The good teacher explains.
The superior teacher demonstrates. The great teacher inspires."
– William Arthur Ward

How to Teach Academic Vocabulary

Conclusion

"Better than 1,000 days of diligent study is one day with a great teacher."

– Japanese Proverb

I want to share a humorous observation that I saw many years ago when my dad was in the Air Force. *(I grew up a military brat.)* I can remember that as we read it, we laughed and loved the idea that every branch of the service had its own vocabulary and special way of talking. To me it epitomizes why language is so important, and I think it really reinforces why we must teach academic vocabulary in every content area.

> *"One reason the services have trouble operating jointly is they don't speak the same language. For example, if you told Navy personnel to secure a building, they would turn off the lights and lock the doors. The Army would occupy the building so no one could enter. Marines would assault the building, capture it, and defend it with suppressive fire and close combat. The Air Force, on the other hand, would take a three-year lease with an option to buy."*
>
> *– Armed Forces Journal, September 1989*

Like the branches of the military, every content area has its own academic vocabulary, and if we want our students to be successful in school, we must give them the tools to understand academic vocabulary in each subject. In addition, we had better look at the commonalities of the vocabulary across grade levels and subject areas; teachers must focus on selecting those critical terms and concepts to teach across the board.

A Quick Review

Some Guiding Principles for Teaching Vocabulary

- Preteach key terms to improve comprehension: Readers are able to tolerate text in which as many as 15 percent of the words are not known.

- It's beneficial to teach new words systematically over a long period of time.

- Introduce words in related clusters. Interconnectedness makes words easier to learn.

- Employ teaching techniques that stress the connections among related terms like charts, diagrams, and thematic approaches.

- Provide more than definitions. Students can memorize definitions, but their knowledge of terms presented this way is likely to be superficial and short-lived.

- Link new words to old knowledge. Linking the new with the known is the only way that word meanings will be integrated with prior knowledge so they can be used appropriately.

- Use a combination of definitions and contextual examples. This technique will demonstrate the deeper meanings of words and model correct and incorrect usage.

- Provide for brief, periodic review using activities and games. Occasionally revisiting previously introduced terms in short, intensive review sessions helps ensure long-term retention.

- Maximize the volume of reading that students do. Nagy has called this "the single most important thing a teacher can do to promote vocabulary growth" (1988, p. 38).

- Stress context and structural analysis—the chief tools students need to acquire word meanings as they read. Do all you can to ensure that students attempt to apply these skills as they read independently.

- Be aware of the limitation of definitions. Formal dictionary definitions can be difficult to understand and misleading. They are insufficient as a means of learning new words.

- Minimize rote copying of definitions. Dictionary use is an important skill, but precious time is wasted by having students copy definitions. The tedium involved can be numbing for most students.

"If a child can't learn the way we teach, maybe we should teach the way they learn."

– Ignacio Estrada

Academic Vocabulary Graphic Organizers

The full-size, reproducible graphic organizers that follow are organized sequentially by strategy number.

Vocabulary Placemat

Menu

- new word and definition
- picture or a visual representation of the term
- synonym (a word that means about the same thing)
- the singular or plural of the new word
- how it would look
- a sentence with the word used correctly
- another word in a different language that would mean the same thing
- an antonym (opposite)
- a homonym (a word that sounds like the new word)
- an analogy using the word

BiG IDea circle

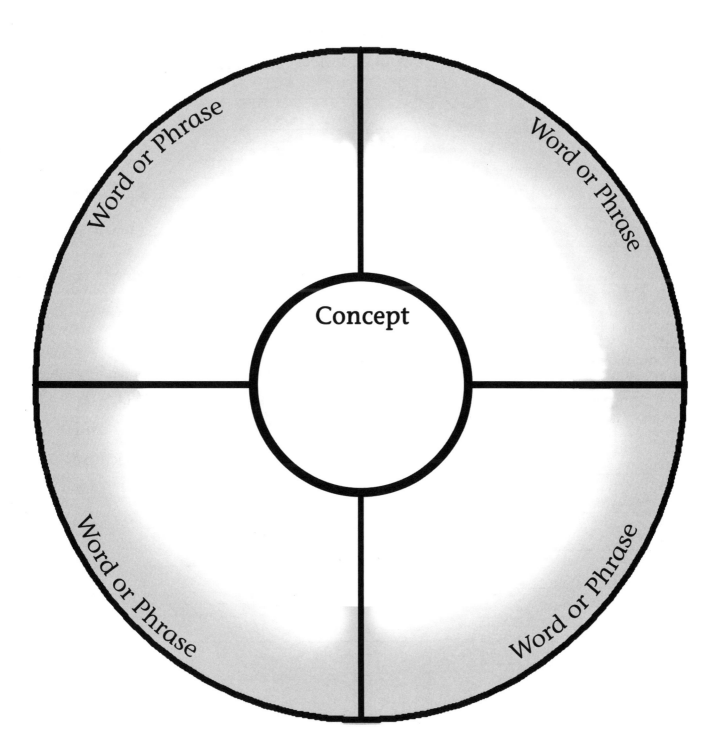

Word or Phrase

Word or Phrase

Concept

Word or Phrase

Word or Phrase

connect Two

Words or Phrases

_____

_____

_____

_____

_____

_____

_____

_____

_____

_____

_____

_____

_____

_____

_____

_____

_____

▶ **Before you read:**

I would connect _____ and

_____ because

_____

_____

I would connect _____ and

_____ because

_____

_____

▶ **After you read:**

BASED ON WHAT I HAVE READ,

I would connect _____ and

_____ because

_____

_____

I would connect _____ and

_____ because

_____

_____

Name _____ Date _____

How to Teach Academic Vocabulary

Name _____

Date _____

On The Other Hand

term or concept

opposing term or concept

YES? or NO?

Definition

Characteristics

Term or Concept

Examples

Nonexamples

yes? or NO?

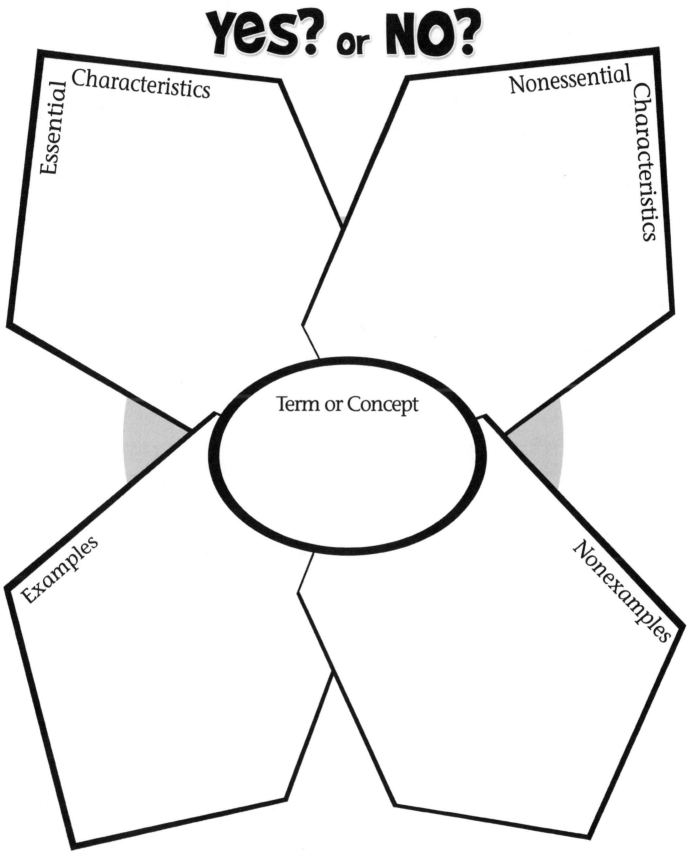

Essential Characteristics

Nonessential Characteristics

Term or Concept

Examples

Nonexamples

How Well Do I Know These WORDS?

✔ Word	✔ I can teach it.	✔ I've heard of it.	✔ This is new to me.

Find someone to teach you one of the words for which you checked the second or third column.

The word someone taught me:

_____

What it means:

_____

_____

_____

A visual image that will help me remember what it means:

Name _____ Date _____

How to Teach Academic Vocabulary

ILLUSTRATE and ASSOCIATE

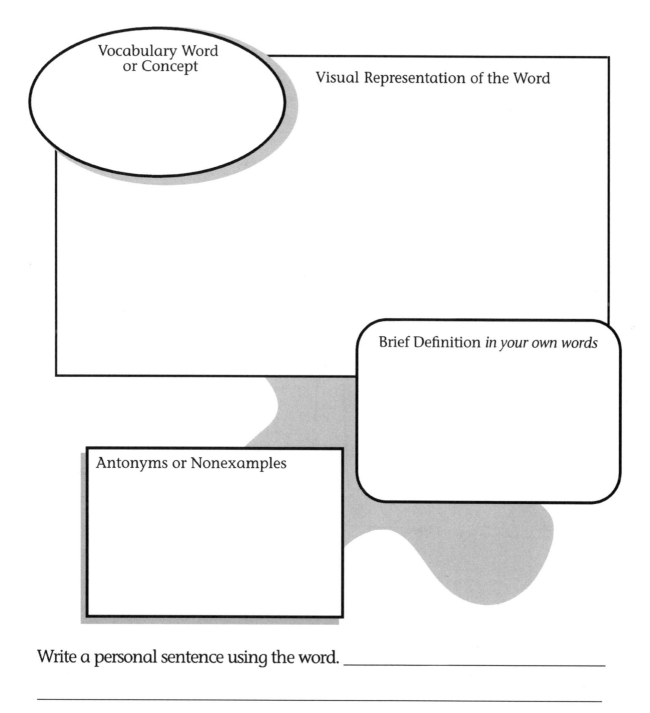

Vocabulary Word
or Concept

Visual Representation of the Word

Brief Definition *in your own words*

Antonyms or Nonexamples

Write a personal sentence using the word. _____

_____

_____

LIST, GROUP, LABEL

Topic _____

My List of Terms

_____ _____ _____ _____

_____ _____ _____ _____

_____ _____ _____ _____

_____ _____ _____ _____

_____ _____ _____ _____

GrouP 1

Label: _____

GrouP 2

Label: _____

GrouP 3

Label: _____

GrouP 4

Label: _____

Name: _____ Date: _____

How to Teach Academic Vocabulary
©Copyright Incentive Publications, Inc., Nashville, TN

Puzzle It!

Big Idea or Topic: _____

P.A.V.E. the way!

the word:

PREDICT

Tell what you think the word means.

Write a sentence showing your predicted meaning.

ASSOCIATE

Find the word in the text and write that sentence here.

VERIFY

Check the meaning of the word in a dictionary or glossary. Write the definition that fits the meaning of the word as it is used in the sentence from the text.

EVALUATE

Compare the dictionary meaning of the word with your predicted meaning. Judge your initial prediction.

Was your prediction correct?

Why do you think your prediction was or was not correct?

If your first sentence did not predict the word meaning correctly, write a new sentence.

Name _____ Date _____

How to Teach Academic Vocabulary
©Copyright Incentive Publications, Inc., Nashville, TN

on **Close** InsPection

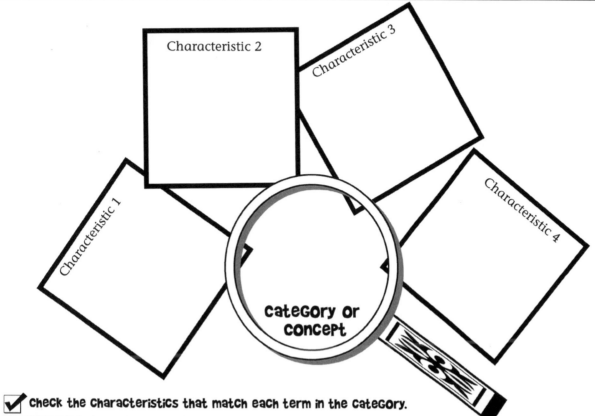

✓ CheCk the CharaCteristics that match each term in the CateGory.

Key Terms	Characteristic 1	Characteristic 2	Characteristic 3	Characteristic 4

Name _____ Date _____

WORDS on a SCALE

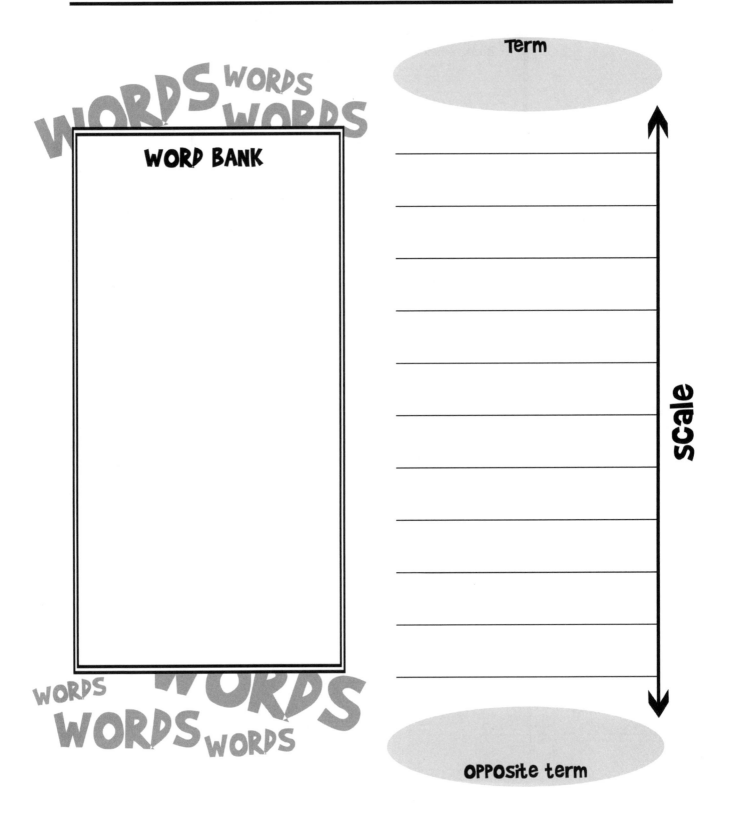

WORDS WORDS WORDS WORDS

WORD BANK

Term

Scale

WORDS WORDS WORDS WORDS WORDS

opposite term

Name _____ Date _____

The **CLUNK** Bus

Definition: _____

_____

Definition: _____

_____

TIP – Term, Information, Picture

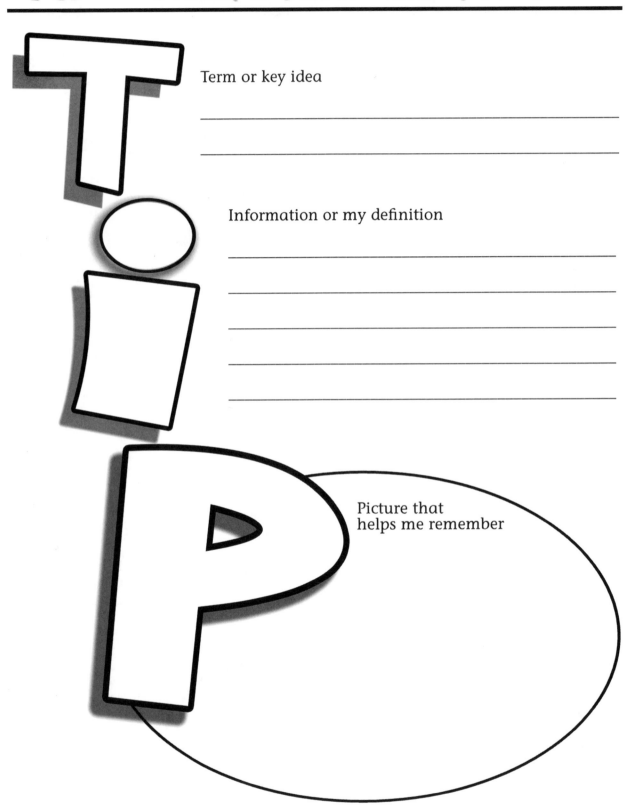

Term or key idea

_____

_____

Information or my definition

_____

_____

_____

_____

_____

Picture that
helps me remember

It's in the Cards

Big Idea or Term

Predict the definition using what you already know

Dictionary or glossary definition

Dictionary or glossary definition in your own words

A visual representation of the word that hints at its meaning

Name _____ Date _____

Name _____ Date _____

It's PREDiCtaBLe!

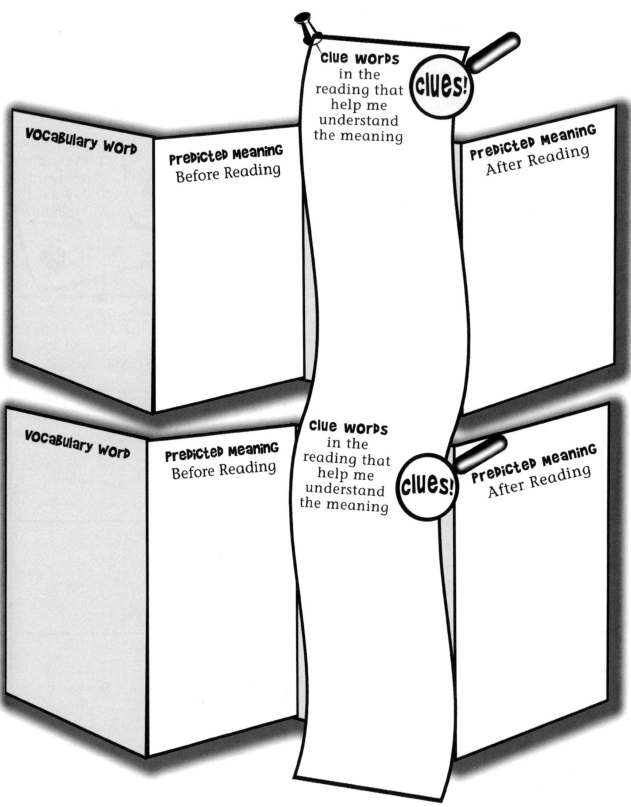

VOCABULARY WORD

PREDiCTED MEANING
Before Reading

CLUE WORDS
in the
reading that
help me
understand
the meaning

clues!

PREDiCTED MEANING
After Reading

VOCABULARY WORD

PREDiCTED MEANING
Before Reading

CLUE WORDS
in the
reading that
help me
understand
the meaning

clues!

PREDiCTED MEANING
After Reading

How to Teach Academic Vocabulary
©Copyright Incentive Publications, Inc., Nashville, TN

FiCtiON PreDictiONS

WORD BANK

SettiNG
Which words does the author use to describe the setting?

CharacterS
Which words can help you make predictions about the characters?

CONfliCt
Which words help describe the conflict?

Plot
Which words help predict what will happen in the story?

ResolutiON
Which words suggest something about the story's resolution?

QuestiONS
Based on the words in the Word Bank, what questions do you have about this story?

? MYStery WOrDS ?
Words that seem important, but you don't yet know why

WORD BANK

NONFICTION PREDICTIONS

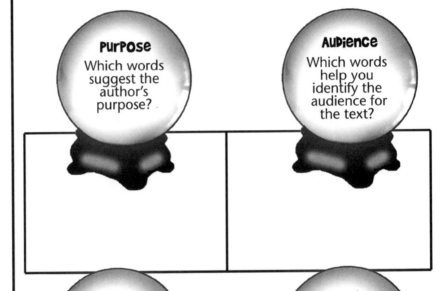

PURPOSE
Which words suggest the author's purpose?

AUDIENCE
Which words help you identify the audience for the text?

MAIN IDEA
Which words point to the main idea of the selection?

SUPPORTING FACTS
Which words help identify facts to support a point or argument?

MYSTERY WORDS
Words that seem important, but you don't yet know why

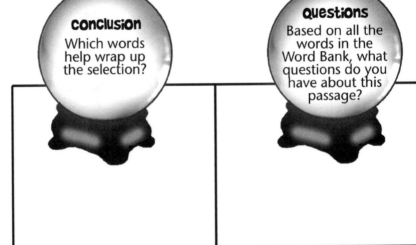

CONCLUSION
Which words help wrap up the selection?

QUESTIONS
Based on all the words in the Word Bank, what questions do you have about this passage?

How to Teach Academic Vocabulary
©Copyright Incentive Publications, Inc., Nashville, TN

WORD BANK

NONFICTION PREDICTION

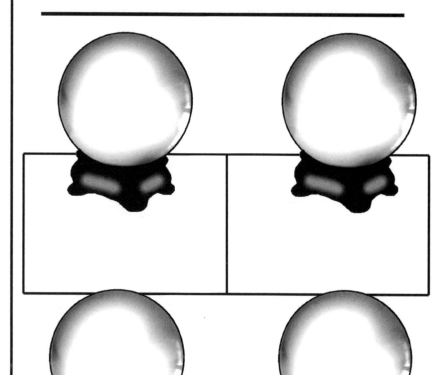

?

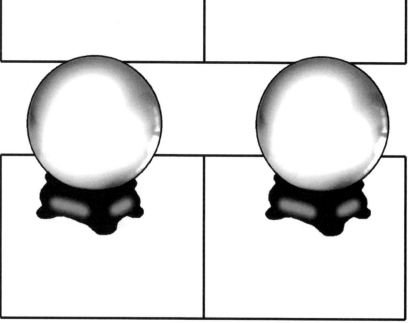

WOrD SPiral

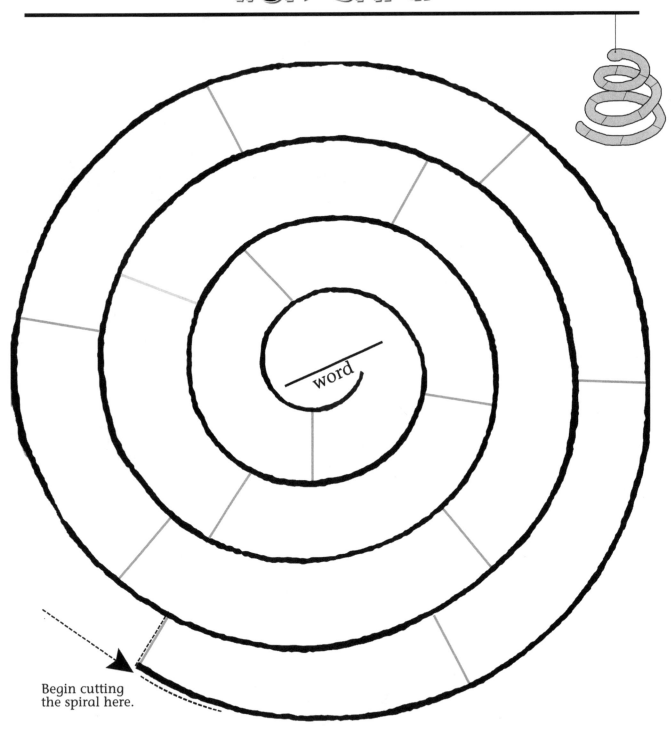

word

Begin cutting
the spiral here.

Name _____ Date _____

How to Teach Academic Vocabulary

Words Take Flight

Show that you know the meanings of words and have fun making words fly!

Directions:

1. Write your word on the long section between solid lines 1 and 2.

2. Cut on all the dotted lines.

3. Fold BACKWARD on solid lines 1, 2, and 3.

4. Fold FORWARD on solid lines 4 and 5.

5. Decorate the helicopter lightly.

6. Hold it high in the air and let it drop. Watch it whirl and twirl.

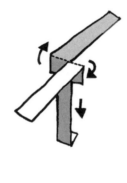

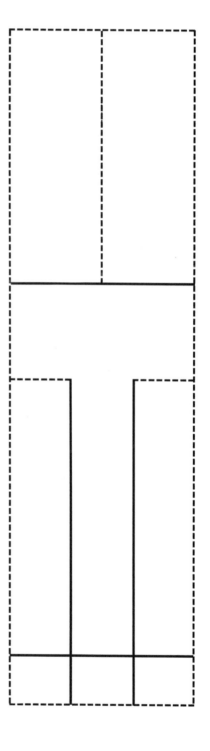

WONDER wheel

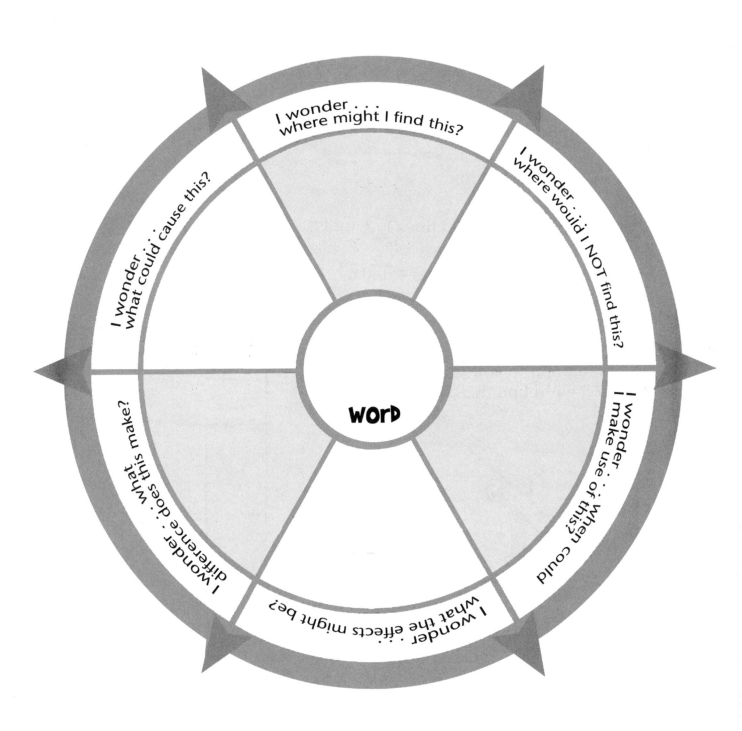

Name _____ Date _____

How to Teach Academic Vocabulary

Name _____ Date _____

DIGGING DEEPER

THE WORD _____

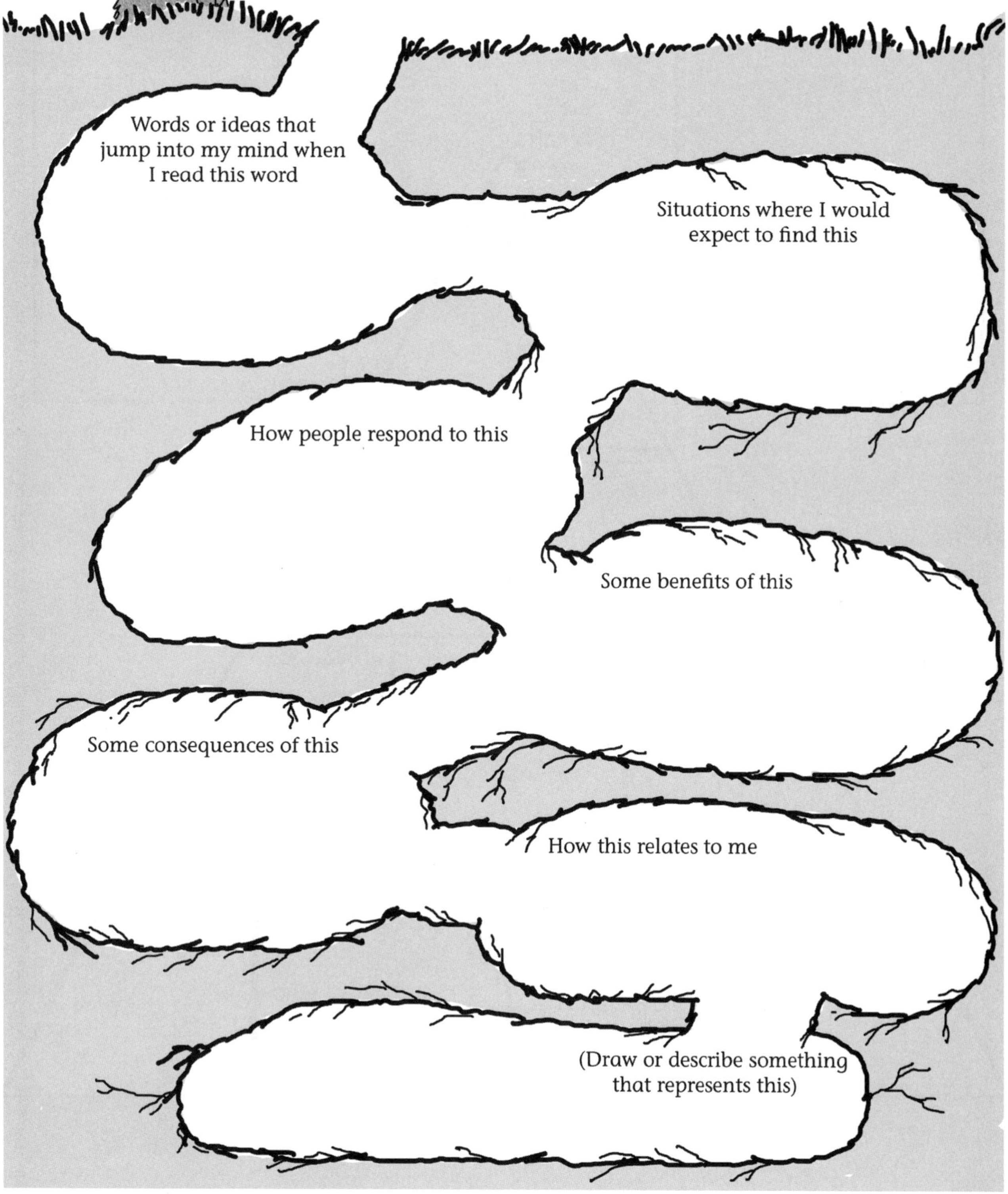

Words or ideas that jump into my mind when I read this word

Situations where I would expect to find this

How people respond to this

Some benefits of this

Some consequences of this

How this relates to me

(Draw or describe something that represents this)

Name _____ Date _____

VOCaBulary PyramiD

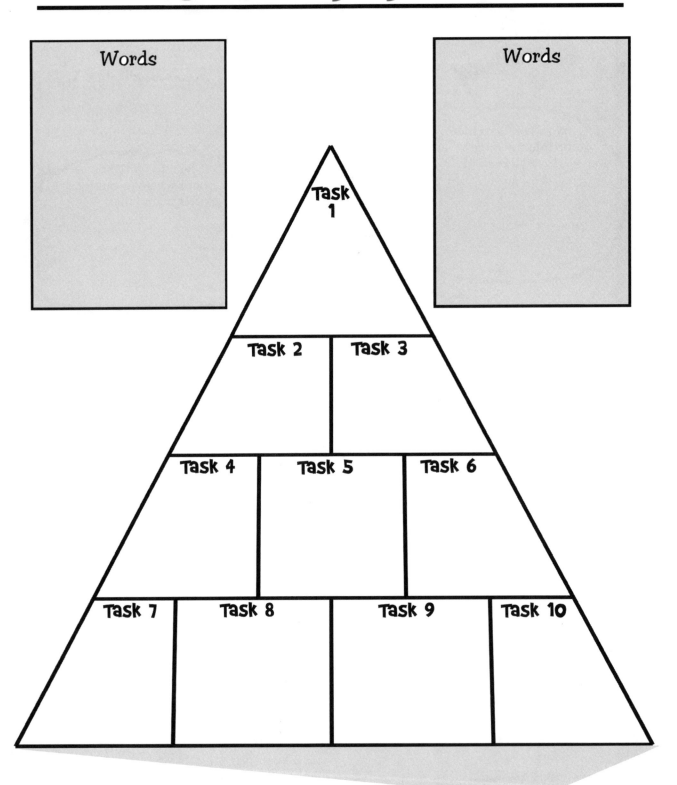

Words

Words

Task 1

Task 2

Task 3

Task 4

Task 5

Task 6

Task 7

Task 8

Task 9

Task 10

VOCaBuLary PyramiD

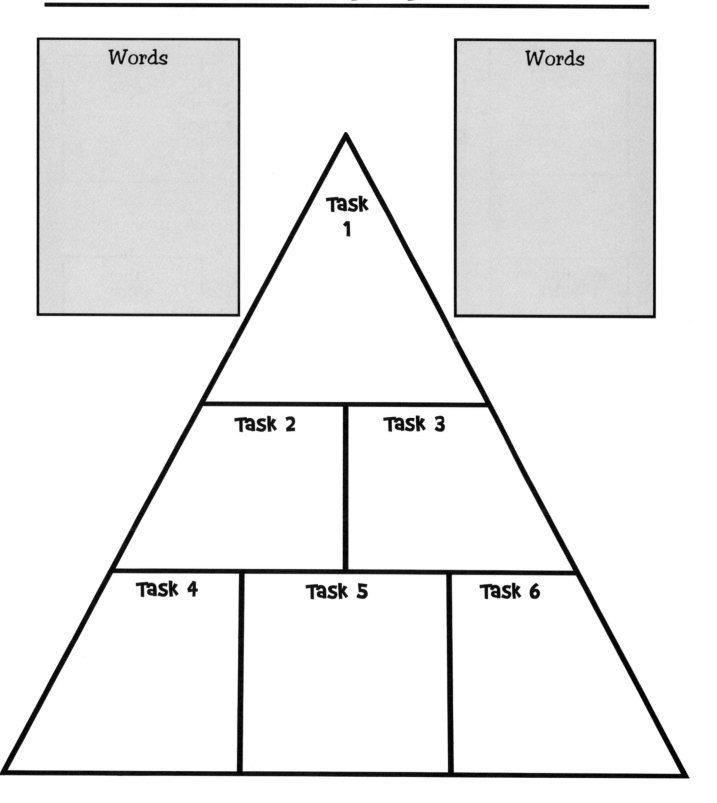

Words

Words

Task 1

Task 2   Task 3

Task 4   Task 5   Task 6

Name _____ Date _____

Unlocking Analogies

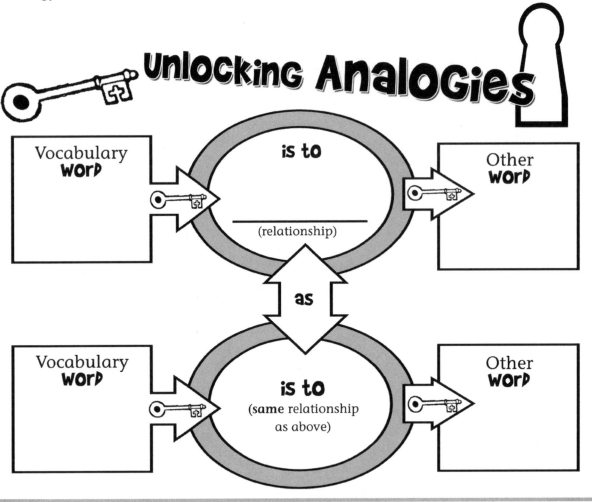

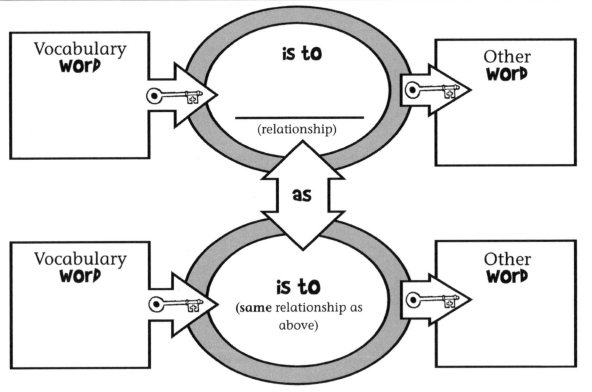

Name _____ Date _____

word Map

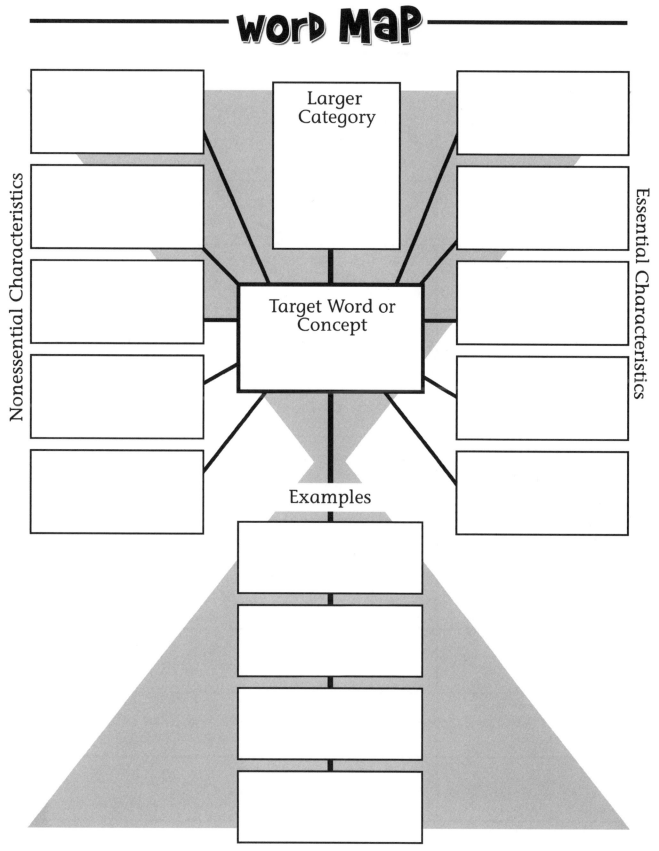

Larger
Category

Nonessential Characteristics

Essential Characteristics

Target Word or
Concept

Examples

Name _____ Date _____

WORD CACHE

WORDS	Why?

The WORD storm —

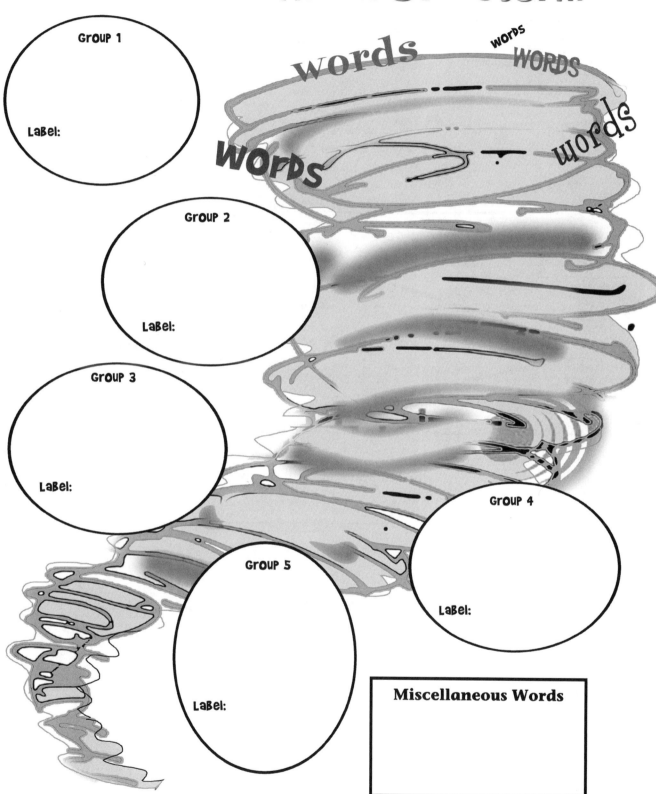

Group 1

Label:

Group 2

Label:

Group 3

Label:

Group 4

Label:

Group 5

Label:

Miscellaneous Words

Name _____ Date _____

WORD SPLASH

Use all the words in a sentence (or two) that gives your idea
of what the passage will be about.

_____

_____

_____

How did your idea change after you read?

How to Teach Academic Vocabulary
©Copyright Incentive Publications, Inc., Nashville, TN

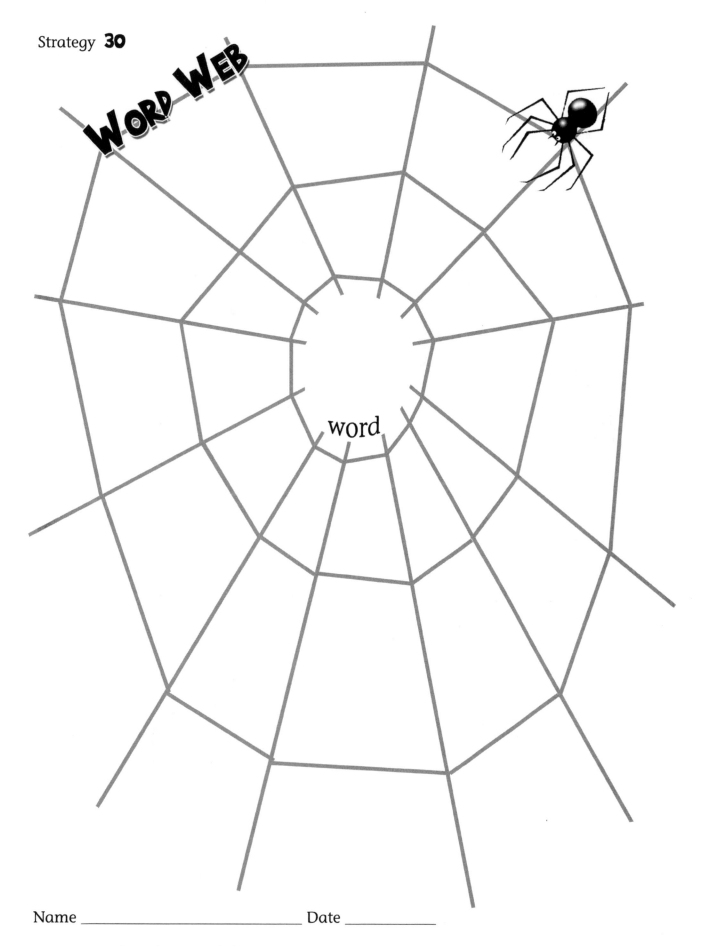

WORD WEB

word

Name _____

Date _____

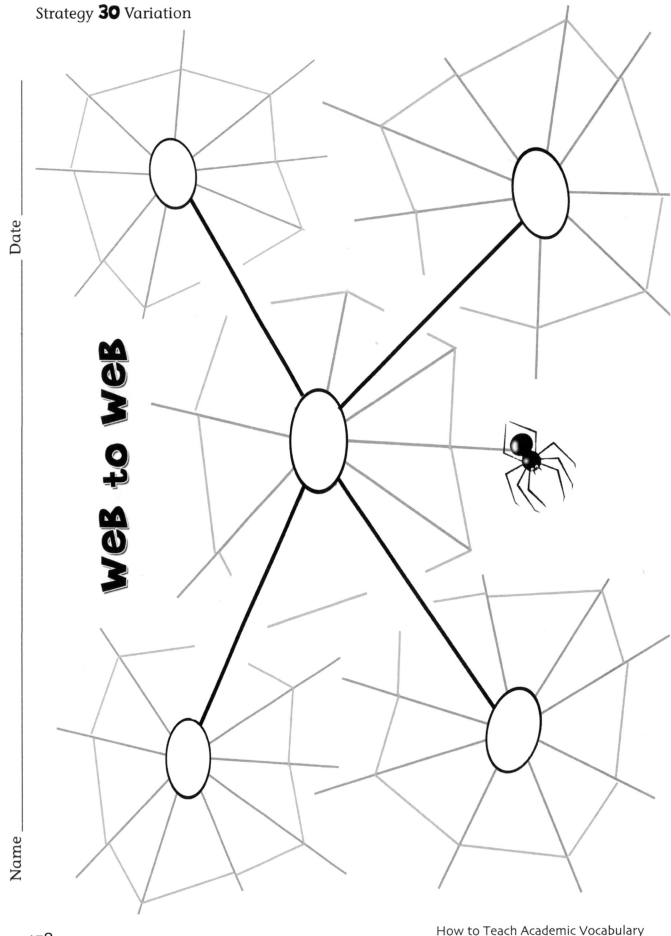

weB to weB

ABC VocaBulary Review

A	J	S
B	K	T
C	L	U
D	M	V
e	n	W
F	o	X
G	P	y
H	Q	Z
I	R	

Summary

ABC voCaBulary ReVIEW

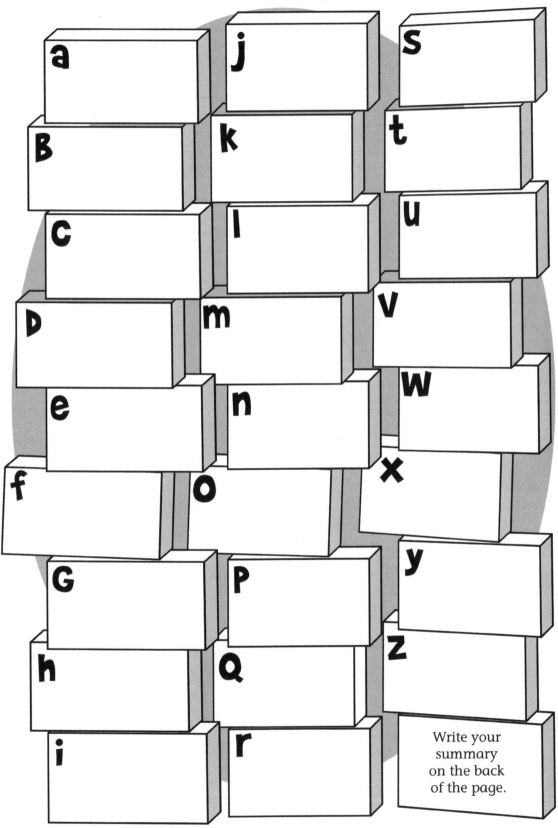

a

B

C

D

e

f

G

h

i

j

k

l

m

n

o

P

Q

r

s

t

u

v

w

x

y

z

Write your
summary
on the back
of the page.

Name _____ Date _____

CuBe Pattern

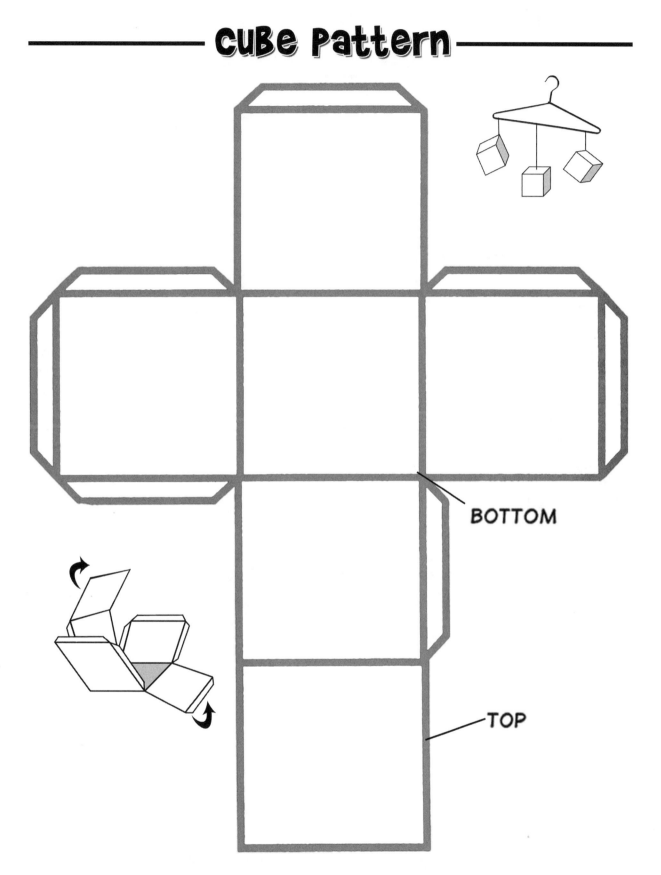

BOTTOM

TOP

Name _____ Date _____

Greet and GO

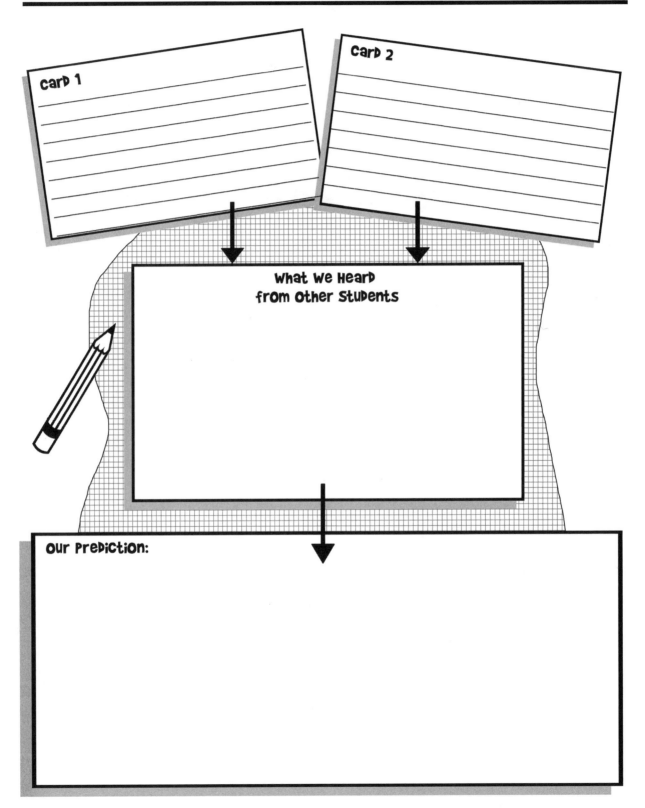

CarD 1

CarD 2

What We Heard
from Other Students

Our PreDiction:

Name _____ Date _____

In the Fast Lane

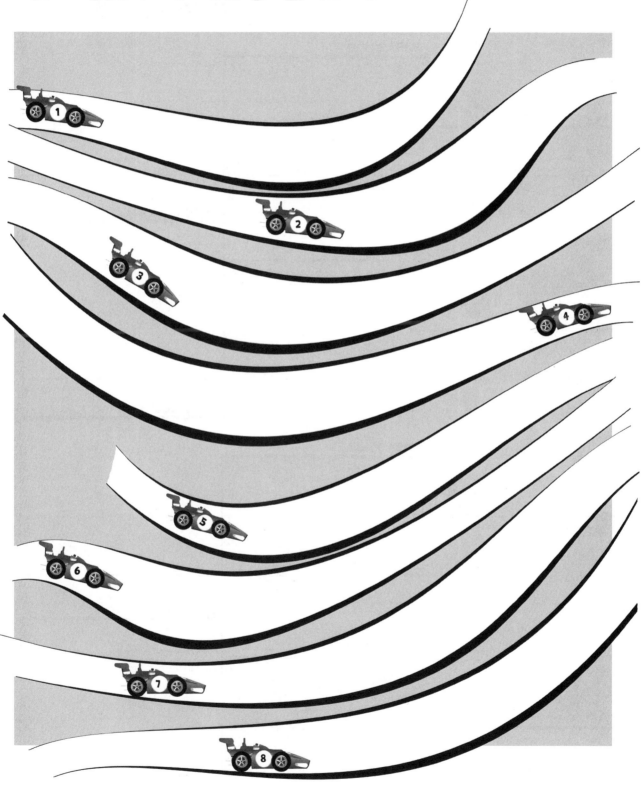

Name _____ Date _____

The Connotation Step-Up

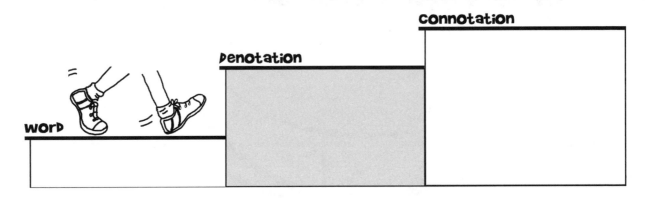

Word   Denotation   connotation

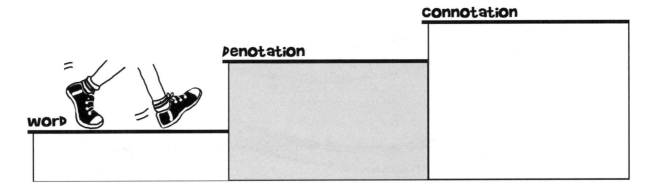

Word   Denotation   connotation

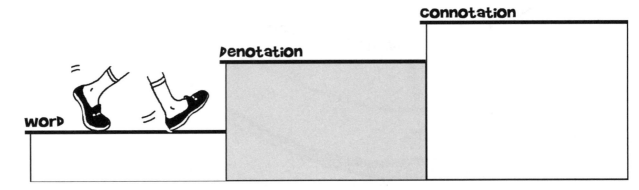

Word   Denotation   connotation

Word   Denotation   connotation

How to Teach Academic Vocabulary
©Copyright Incentive Publications, Inc., Nashville, TN

Pattern for Looping Cards

Start I have Who has	I have Who has
I have Who has	I have Who has
I have Who has	I have Who has
I have Who has	I have Who has **Stop!**

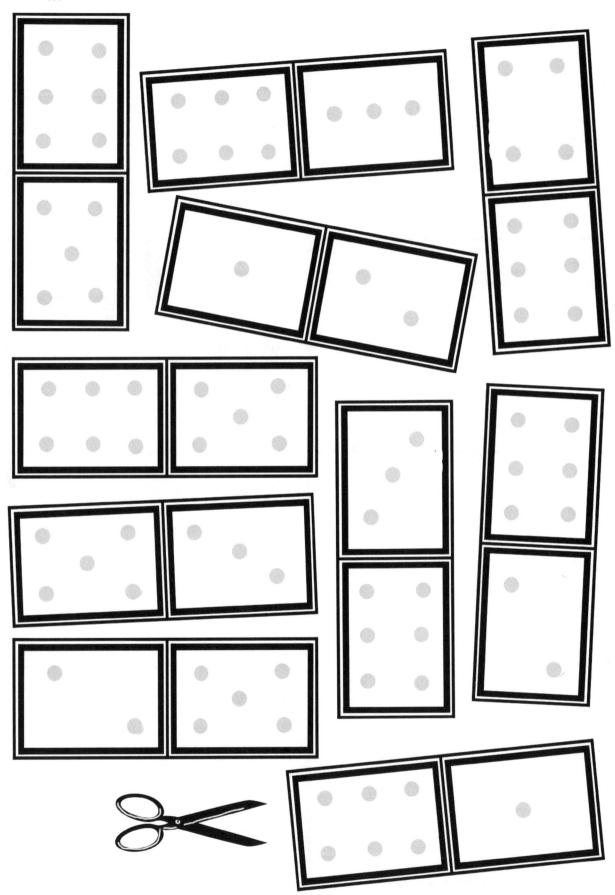

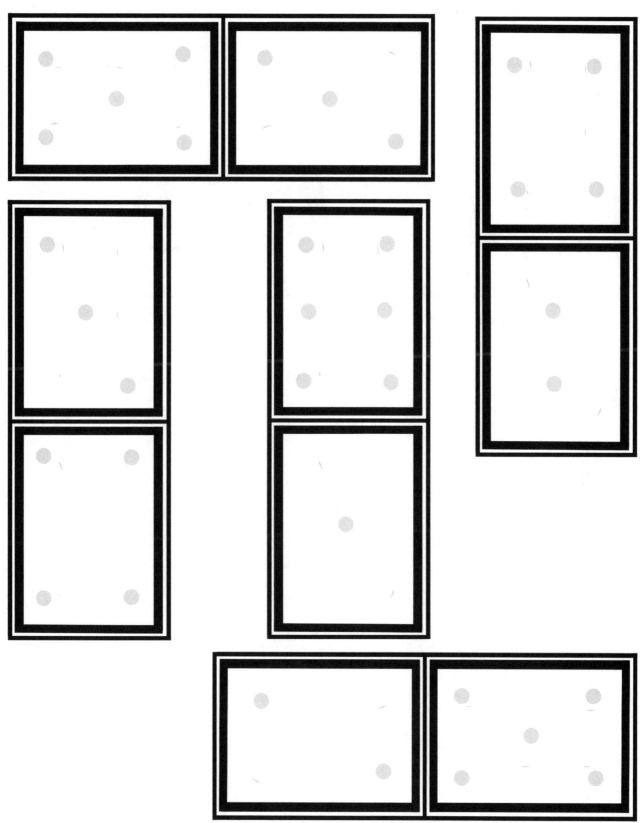

Name _____ Date _____

In your OWN words

New Words

What I Think
This Is About

Clues and Details that Help Me Understand
the New Words and Ideas

My Paraphrase

How to Teach Academic Vocabulary
©Copyright Incentive Publications, Inc., Nashville, TN

Word Part Sort

Word Part (root, Prefix, or suffix)	Meaning	Examples
ab	away from	
able	capable of, worthy of	
ad	to, toward	
ance, ence, ancy, ency	act or fact of doing, state, quality	
audio	to hear	
cap	to seize, take, or contain	
co, con, com, col, cor	together, with	
de	away, down, out of	
dis	not, opposite	
er, or	person or thing connected with	
ex	out of, formerly	
ful	full of, abounding in	
in, im, il, ir in,	not	
inter	between	
less	without, free from	
ly	like, characteristic of	
ment	state of, quality of	
meter	measure	
mis	wrong	
phon	sound, speech	
pre	before	
pro	forward	
re	back, again	
spect, spec, spic	to observe, watch	
sub	under	
tele	distance	
tion, sion, xion	action, state, result	
trans	across or beyond	
un	not, opposite	
vid, vis	to see or look at	

3 **Facts** AND **1** **Fib**

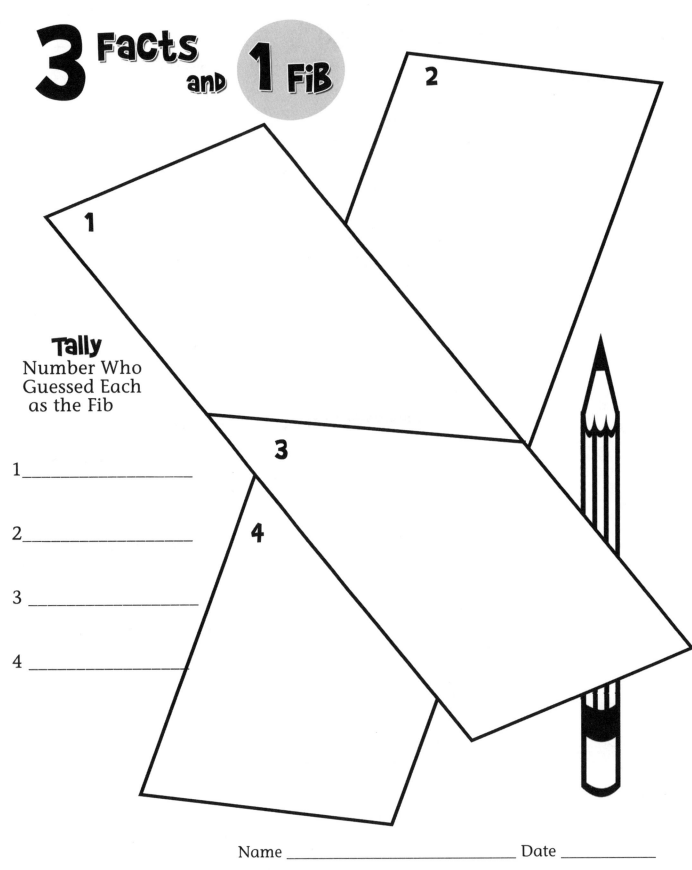

Tally
Number Who
Guessed Each
as the Fib

1_____

2_____

3 _____

4 _____

Name _____ Date _____

How to Teach Academic Vocabulary

Name _____ Date _____

on TarGet!

ExPlain three of the associations:

1. I Chose _____ Because _____

2. I Chose _____ Because _____

3. I Chose _____ Because _____

Follow the Clues

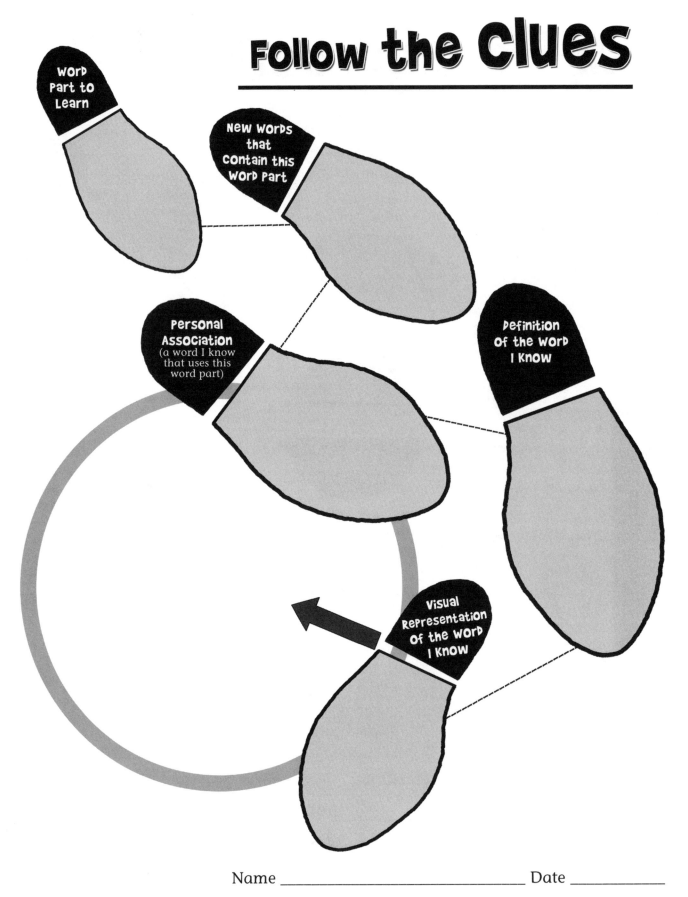

WORD
Part to
Learn

New Words
that
Contain this
WORD Part

Personal
Association
(a word I know
that uses this
word part)

Definition
Of the WORD
I Know

Visual
Representation
Of the Word
I Know

Name _____ Date _____

How to Teach Academic Vocabulary

Name _____ Date _____

Name That Category!

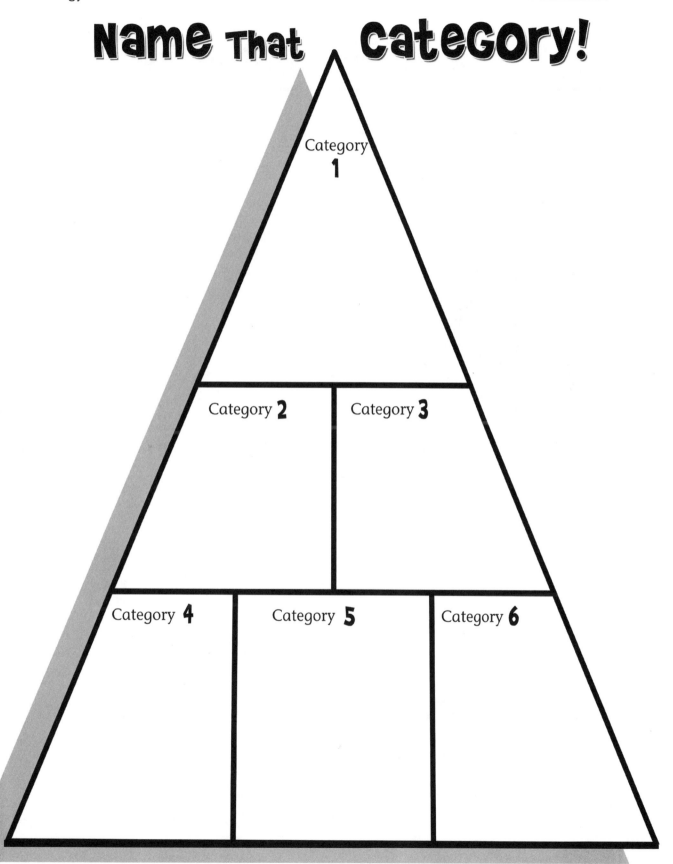

Category **1**

Category **2**   Category **3**

Category **4**   Category **5**   Category **6**

VocaBulary HiP-HOP

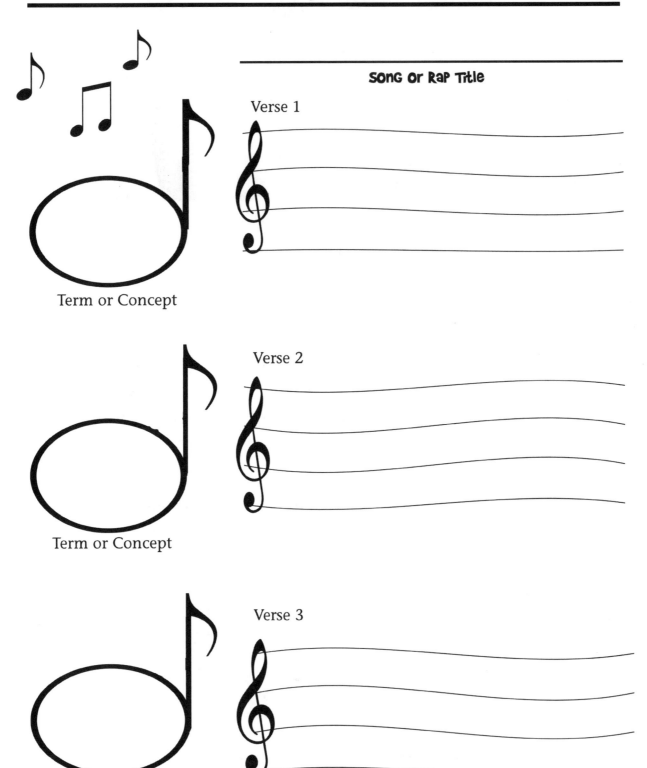

SonG or RaP Title

Verse 1

Term or Concept

Verse 2

Term or Concept

Verse 3

Term or Concept

Name _____ Date _____

VOCaBuLary-O

VO	CAB	U	LARY	-O